To Marvin,

Just Thankful,

Sonny

REFLECTIONS OF AN ARMY CHAPLAIN

From Sonny to Reverend Davis to Chaplain Davis
to Dr. Davis to Sonny-Just Tell the Truth

DR . ELVERNICE "SONNY" DAVIS

WESTBOW
PRESS®
A DIVISION OF THOMAS NELSON
& ZONDERVAN

WestBow Press books may be ordered through booksellers or by contacting:

WestBow Press
A Division of Thomas Nelson & Zondervan
1663 Liberty Drive
Bloomington, IN 47403
www.westbowpress.com
1 (866) 928-1240

Scripture taken from the King James Version of the Bible.

ISBN: 978-1-9736-8823-5 (sc)
ISBN: 978-1-9736-8825-9 (hc)
ISBN: 978-1-9736-8824-2 (e)

Library of Congress Control Number: 2020904664

Print information available on the last page.

WestBow Press rev. date: 3/26/2020

CONTENTS

PREFACE AND ACKNOWLEDGEMENT

This book could not have been completed and published without the encouragement, professional input and enabling emotional stability by my spouse, Cynthia. Many crucial supporters include our children, Carrel, Calandra, Jocelyn and Derrick who provided my reasons for continued living when times in war and peace became seemingly overbearing. I quoted my parents throughout my book: father B. F. and mother M.L. Davis, who paid for our pre-kindergarten schooling and emphasized the importance of education. I also thank our older sister Rubye (Suge) for forcing me to return to college, with fully paid tuition, after skipping my first year out of high school. All ten siblings have at least four years of college, assisted in many ways by Rubye. Many white and black angels "unawares" were placed in my pathway and mentioned as such throughout this book. This lifework is a network of gifts by friends, too many to list, and without whom I would not be. I thank God for allowing them to enable me to be whatever I am. Since African American (AA) is a current acceptable term for Black Americans (BA), I have used the terms interchangeably, depending on the context.

As an army chaplain for 30 years, I had opportunity to work with and serve as pastor of the world community of God's greatest creation. I never felt called to be a neighborhood pastor though I loved it, equally as well.

Reflections of an Army Chaplain are just that. The book is a composite of written and resurfaced experiences and not always in chronological order. I apologize to the many friends who at varied stages of my development encouraged me to publish my thoughts. I further apologize for criticizing the many graduate and post-graduate level professors whose uniquely inspired presentations were not put in print. *Placing thoughts in print is not only difficult but so easily debatable, when in group blindness, individuals attempt describing the body of an elephant.* In spirit, for whatever justification, I was not ready to publish until today. So, you get the whole load. Whoever you are, I love you in Christ. I unconditionally love you. That's also my Calling and practiced position in life. Thanks for sharing your time while permitting me to unload on you.

My goal is consistent: Respect our U.S. flag and Constitution *of our USA* for whom Americans have fought and died protecting; The Christian faith, at its core, not necessarily in its practice, *is* not the only world religion but the one, I believe, has the best hope for establishing world peace. *(In this I am like the Apostle Peter in response to the question of Jesus asking during the withdrawal of the Disciples- "Lord to whom shall we go? Thou hast the words of eternal life." (John 6:67-68, KJV)*

It is not intended as a scholarly masterpiece though it reveals respect for academia. Yet some scholarly classified works of academia may be the primary cause of contemporary tragic social consequences. This book is inclusive of 79 years of living.

I don't want to be misunderstood. I am an American of color. American of color and was first born and raised in, appointed to American churches for eight years and loved it. Inhabitants of my community of origin were to make me who I am in experiences and education, from kindergarten through high school, college and seminary. Americans of color are my parents, my siblings, my extended family, my best friends, my dates, my marriage, my children. The concepts of neighborhood and community refer to locations where people are appointed or choose to live.

A *neighborhood* is defined by Wikipedia as a geographically localized community within a larger city, town suburb or rural area. Usually the people in neighborhoods have shared beliefs, political alignment, churches, etc. Wikipedia contends that definitions of community are vague. At Long Island University, Brooklyn, NY, where I received a Master of Arts Degree in Sociology, *community* was differentiated as a group of neighborhoods in a geographically identified area but whose culture and social constraints within the neighborhoods may differ.

When I preached my first sermon, the Spirit *of our Lord* led me to *the Book of* Jonah. Jonah as a prophet was willing and comfortable preaching to the neighborhood but unwilling to preach to the community. *In language of today,* the folks in the neighborhood, were where the guys told jokes at the barber shop, felt compatible with their genealogy, went to schools and religious gatherings with families and folks that also looked like them.

They knew other folks occupied their earth and developed their own bias about their looks, attitudes toward strangers, desires and behaviors. Like their ancestors, they built walls, physical and imaginary for their protection. They, perhaps, also felt that when their neighborhood supplies got low or they became adventurous, it was ok to overpower other communities and bring the spoils back to their *neighborhood.* It was perceivably much easier and safer and productive to go out into other *neighborhoods* for conquest than deal with the emotional backlash and critique of neighbors.

Let me insert here that rather than the neighborhood, it appears that even God's Call to Abraham was to "Get thee out of thy country, *(neighborhood)* and from your kindred, and from thy father's house, unto a land that I will show thee:" (Genesis 12: 1,KJV). God's spirit carried Peter to a house top experience what I have called a sociological purification (Acts 10:9-15, KJV). Sociological purification because his experience dealt with inter-neighborhood representations rather than a *homogenized community*. Even God seemingly waited for the community to be together, in Jerusalem, before the Pentecost celebration of Acts 2, (the world baptism of the Holy Spirit). Chaplain (COL) Conrad Walker emphasized to me that Acts 2, *or the biblical story of* Pentecost should be a Race Relations Celebration *in all* American churches because of God's divine act of baptizing diversity (community).

Growth, whether spiritual or physical requires expansion and therefore also requires a base of community, not restricted, socially anemic neighborhood solidarity, which under duress, snaps to *social* smithereens.

As an army chaplain, it saddens me to remember soldiers of Vietnam, of which I was one, who fought and died under our American flag for others to live under the American flag in peace. I have long since forgotten the names of soldiers I memorialized on the battlefield and in family funerals, but I shall never forget their races and spirit, and many of their faces. They died fighting for our American flag of freedom. And tragically, here today, 2019, *I experience* America is still dealing with the *historical* issues of denying its citizens equal rights to vote, decent housing, comparable education, the right to decent wages, respect, healthcare and in many incidentals, to the right to life. *An equally disturbing trend, through the burning of Jewish synagogues, Moslem mosques and Christian churches with terroristic murdering; or threats to control contents of their beliefs, an infringement on the rights of freedom of religion, all are worst nightmares for a world leading country of democratic beliefs.*

I began this book with the poems that follow which were written by me in Vietnam during some terrible emotional crises. Additionally, I decided to share in this book personal experiences with wonderful people over against classic scholastic research, which is abundant for those whose scholarly interest is greater than mine. As your feelings may also be pinched in this reading, I hope you can feel my pain, as well as sense a release from guilt in dealing with God, neighbors and self.

The poems you are about to hear or read were inspired after the renowned TET II offensive where the North Vietnam leaders struck our forces with an intensive, all-out battle strategy to bring South Vietnam under psychological domination. During that intensity, history demonstrates that our soldiers and their allies responded valiantly throughout each battle site. I served in Vietnam from November 1968 until October 1969 and the war would continue until 1975.

As a junior ranking chaplain, I was given a unique opportunity in assignment to the 4th Infantry Division Headquarters. Due to rising racial problems. Chaplain (COL) Gerhardt Hyatt, V CORPS Chaplain, said *to me* the Commanding General, Major General Charles P. Stone, had requested an African American Chaplain for the 4th Infantry Division to assist resolution for these racial tensions. He was promised the next African American Chaplain assigned to Vietnam.

In my orientation at Headquarters, United States Army V CORPS Chaplains Office, I was told I was the first assigned black chaplain in six months, so I was being assigned because of my race. My request was for assignment to Cam Ram Bay where my younger brother, Lestine, was assigned to the *Cam Ram Bay Airforce* base adjacent to the army post.

However, the assignment proved providential for me. With only thirteen months in the army, at our division combat headquarters I was given opportunity to travel throughout our massive II CORPS area in the Central Highlands of South Vietnam; attend division headquarters briefings on division strategies, combat losses, troop morale, logistical issues, tactical mishaps and senior command tensions. I co-led and led worship services at the division headquarters, combat units without assigned chaplains and along with the Division Chaplain, Chaplain (LTC) Von Lemming, visited other combat chaplains and soldiers in their assigned field locations. Several times, before assignment to a military squadron, I provided spiritual meditations on closed circuit television which were televised throughout our command. I also provided spiritual leadership to a Montagnard Village outside our Division Headquarters at Pleiku.

Additionally, I was assigned for Protestant Chaplain coverage to our Pleiku Fourth Evacuation Hospital where the wounded and dying were given chances for life and the medical staff was overwhelmed with combat casualties. In addition, the Division Chaplain assigned me to provide counseling to a high volume of soldiers who sought personal support for dealing with issues ranging from marriage stress; "Dear John" letters; perceived racially discriminatory practices in their command; religious issues or simply, battle fatigue.

My assignment further entailed briefing the Commander, through the Division Chaplain, with information leading to causes for racial strife in the command. In this position I experienced, along with myself, the black soldier always had another battle to fight – the psychological war against what is identified as racism. I don't know which experience captivated me the most at the time of this writing: The Civil Rights Movement going on in the U.S., of which I was a participant; counseling young soldiers affected by accused overt racial acts inflicted upon them by their *uniformed peers and commanding officers;* watching black soldiers fight and die from battle, in the midst of racial insensitivity, or suffering the indignities of little things such as lack of needed black products in the Post Exchanges.

In the Post Exchanges, among Stars and Stripes, Time, Newsweek, Esquire, etc., there was a predominance of only white, girly sex magazines. In the U.S., blacks were lynched for pursuing their sexual desires with the same, either physically or visionary. Yet in Vietnam, the only sexual media images available for blacks, whites, South Vietnamese and other supportive countries, *were* these images which instilled a sexual hunger for already exploited white female bodies. Capital gain was the obvious business objective, but a second intended or unintended strategy, was felt *by me and other black officers* in conversation, to support white supremacy.

On my visits to the 2/1 Calvary Squadron who also protected Highway 14E bridge sites for our supply carrying convoys, I always collected left over postal subscriptions, letters of commendation to soldiers, candies, and sheet cakes for our young black and white soldiers on the bridge sites. There were always soldiers with uplifted morale waiting to see the chaplain. My Chaplain Assistant and I drove many miles each week providing field worship services to these teenage and over soldiers giving their lives defending, what was *commonly* briefed to us, "Our families and our way of life.

North Vietnamese soldiers, presumably, found such abundant materials discarded by our soldiers in the jungles and abandoned firebases. A naked female, white, black, Vietnamese, Chinese, Korean, European, Indian, etc., is a female with sexual attraction by males of any race. The exploitation of female bodies for financial, political or social gain only complicates the emotional psyche of males and females from every race and culture. Such actions only fostered a developing unhealthy psyche for young soldiers in Vietnam, and as in other American wars, for their return to the United States.

Another example of conscious or unconscious white skin images surfaced in the August 11, 1969 Stars and Stripes newspaper. This was the only official newspaper available to our soldiers. I read an article after a counseling session with a black soldier who was dealing with his realities of racial bias; and another whose hand I held while he died at the Pleiku Hospital. The article was pleading for Southeast Asia to bear her own responsibilities. *"No more will the G.I., with his white skin, bear the brunt end of the fighting."* No reference was made to the black or other non-white soldier's contributions, despite the high percentages of black soldiers in direct combat related units, wounds and death. Rhetoric establishes a truth that, "a picture means more than a thousand words." *For me,* an emotional picture was painted in script.

From these developing social issues, I experienced a battle fatigue from what James Baldwin emphasized in his book, "Nobody Knows my Name." Memories included my attendance in 1968 of my United Methodist General Conference. I was in dress uniform and sat down next to a fellow black clergy. He immediately stood and protested: "I refuse to sit by a *black preacher ("racial slur")* who supports America's war in Vietnam while my black people suffer in America and are even denied the right to vote." He didn't even know my name. I would have discussed how his Pastor's Salary was provided by church members, *uniformed and civilian,* who worked in systems that resourced supplies for the war effort. It was inescapable for any Americans to avoid participation in the war effort. I was there, representing his church *denomination,* because American soldiers, even from his church, were fighting, grieving and dying.

In my travels throughout the division, I reported to my *Supervisory Chaplain* the absence of Jet and Ebony magazines in the Post Exchanges while there were Penthouse, Playboy and Husler magazines. Plus, there were always sexual novels with naked drawings of white women on the covers, yet no equal opportunity access for young soldiers to experience the media beauty of other than white women. Moreover, when reading through the content of these available magazines, I concluded that unhealthy sexual mentalities were in wholesale development for many young soldiers who were future war veterans of our country.

Compounded with the instant availability of prostitutes, marijuana and high-quality cocaine in the countryside to our 17 plus year old kids/soldiers of war, *I contended that* the mystique of the combat environment would have an inevitable negative impact on the future folkways and mores of our country. *When the Command wanted our chaplains to scale down the use of psychedelic drugs, I recommended that alcohol be included for its dangerous impact on individuals and families.* In the many discussions with our young soldiers about sexual morality in a land of open availability, for justification, many expressed fears of being killed and dying or severely wounded without the experience of sex. Most of these young heroes were draftees and unmarried. In an attempt to balance the fatal discussion, I would usually ask, "But what if you live?"

When I asked the Exchange managers the rationale for lack of media or shaving supplies for black soldiers, I was told their supplies of Jet and Ebony or Magic shaving power just ran out and they had no orders or suppliers for black sexual girlie magazines. My retort was, *in reading materials,* there should be all or none. My wife had to keep me supplied with Magic shaving power from the states because of inadequate stocks.

Many black soldiers depended upon this depilatory product to protect themselves from shaving bumps. Consequently, from bumpy or alternate bearded faces which increased the opportunity for command harassment of the black soldier; lack of racial balance in Post Exchange products, were added psychological fuel for racial tensions within the black soldier and extended across racial lines in combat units.

Understandably, it was awkward for this chaplain to encourage the distribution of sexually oriented/explicit supplies. But in good faith, in my asking the "APO" to baggage all left over subscriptions and letters, the PX for any supplies they could give; *requesting* the Mess Sergeant for cakes and donuts, the intent in this war zone was to help our soldiers deal with the ultimate human unexplainable of war. (As of then, I am still shedding tears when remembering our young soldiers, black and white who struggled and died, protecting our flag, while dealing with anguish of feeling used for others, especially the ultra-wealthy and draft *dodgers*, to prosper). Yet I knew that *exploitative* images then and even now in the 21ˢᵗ century, are the strongest ally of white supremacy theories.

I *also* know, in reflection, that in spite of racial tensions, thanks to teachings from my father, mother and "village parents," who were black and white in Mississippi, (a state whose outer image was the seat of racial tension, but on the inside were angels white and black) I successfully transcended powerful tension of race as I dealt with the personal crises, wounds and deaths and wounds of all soldiers in my command. I later learned that those psychological, racial and combat wounds became so deeply embedded in my mind and soul that only with the miraculous opportunity of later spiritual and psychotherapy training, I was able to regain a sense of personal balance. Therefore, I am attempting to explain that transformation in this very book, God willing. May God enable the social ultra-right and ultra-left to become transformed into, what Methodist Healthcare *of Memphis, TN* carved out, *as one of* their themes, "The Power of One." One nation under God.

Prior to arrival in Vietnam, emotionally I had thought I would find seasoned, combat hardened soldiers as the ones I enjoyed while watching the TV episodes of "Combat" staring Vic Morrow. Not so. In Vietnam, our heroes were from seventeen-year-old draftees to older seasoned career soldiers. Many Second Lieutenants were right out of college, Officer Candidate School or West Point. These young Commissioned Officers or Enlisted soldiers (Platoon and Squad Leaders) were like my younger brothers that I had hoped by my being in Vietnam would protect from war.

It was difficult for me to see these young, gifted and wonderful gifts of our nation's future generations become battle hardened to fight or/and die like lower orders of nature in the animal kingdom. I think I started this poem after holding the hand of another young American black soldier who died at the Pleiku Hospital.

The poem you are about to hear was a written attempt to maintain my sanity in combat, along with prayer, so that I could be an efficient pastor/counselor to all the soldiers in my assigned command: Black, White, Hispanic, Native American, Jewish, Muslim and even an African native, whose visa problem (according to him during a counseling session with me), availed him for the draft. Yet, don't think Commissioned and Non-Commissioned Offices were exempt from the same anguish; I think deeper than their subordinates, because they had to give the orders and draw up the battle plans. Isn't the racial labeling stupid, evil, time consuming and just sinful? I think it is. Yes, and I am deeply angry to even describe soldiers that way. We were and are Americans. The movie title is correct: "We Were Soldiers." I prefer to just say "the soldiers or *military members* assigned to commands."

Professionally, the chaplain of color had no one, except other American white chaplains, who were/are great peers, (and chaplains of color had no other like chaplains in their command) to deal with the pain and agony of pastoring those under the burden of human frailty. Consequently, these chaplains of that era usually held their frustrations on the inside. Most chaplains, black or white, saw all non-chaplains as members of their parish, and therefore kept their frustrations within.

I went on from Vietnam to spend 30 years as an Army Chaplain: highly decorated, awarded opportunistic assignments; and graciously retired with the rank of Colonel. My success was made possible by inspiration drawn from and support given by tremendous senior white and black chaplains, senior commissioned and warrant officers, white and black; and "the soldiers in the field," i.e., "all soldiers, airmen, sailors and marines (male and female, white and black) in the field." To the soldier and God be the glory!! Amen!!!

"THE DAY I SAW GOD"

I saw God, after they said he was dead, on a firebase in Vietnam

Though war is always tragedy, God's word is clear

When guns sound with a "Bam!"

To see men like animals, dirty as could be

Men who should be in school

They fight for their country any aggressor in sight

In war they must play by the rule

This God that I saw was not a dictator,

enforcing acceptance of his laws

Not even a big judge presiding over the world

Sentencing for every little cause

Wasn't the God I have seen in churches back home

Thought invoked at every plea

But a God as was human, understanding, patient

And one who even cried with me

He saw these young men, these real good

guys, dying from incoming rounds

Young fathers, young brothers, the best of sons

Cringing from mortar sounds

In the day of the spacecraft, trips to the moon

The complexity of IBM's

Couldn't understand what was happening though they served

Not with all the world's church hymns

But don't forget the enemy, the Viet Cong,

God surely made them too

Though they seemed ignorant, not very anxious either

Just doing as forced to do

They had the very young and some of their young girls

The uniqueness of the Orient

Taught to fight Americans, Australians,

South Vietnamese, and Koreans

Fight wherever they went

Though odds were against them –small, ill-

trained but in every way brave

Fed with a philosophy of men, the worst scoundrels and killers

Whoever it was making them slaves

The men who sit back in easy, air-conditioned chairs

Pretending to be their friend

Just like those who maintain world problems

Seeing people as a means to an end

For many the military is their profession but very few loves to kill

Whenever you find that type of soldier

He is certainly mentally ill

They train to conduct missions, to endure

challenges tiresome and rigorous

In national defense and enemy aggression

They must be alert and vigorous

And then you have the volunteers, also those
who couldn't escape the draft
The chaplains, the lawyers, the doctors and nurses
Including the WAC, WAVE and WAF
These are they who make up the military
The Sad Sack or Gomer Pyle
Draftees, lifer, recruit or whatever they are called
They adjust to the style
Oh, the Air Force is really the leisure, or the Navy
On the ocean blue
If you are in the National Guard or Reserves
You may taste the fighting too
These are the men and women our country chose
To go wherever they are sent
To make zero mistakes, to be nothing but the best
Keep down all the accidents
In these faces I saw God, not much different
from the paintings of Christ
In the chapels, on many firebases
Praying somehow, we could prevent the strife
Men who cried over the death of an enemy
Grief stricken at the loss of a friend
Human emotions didn't seem any different
Then when the teachings of God did begin
Interrogation reports we read, whatever
Intelligence could find to reveal
Though language barriers were different
A supernatural being the enemy could feel
A being responsible for all creation
Though mysterious nobody could explain

Whether to live or death is better

Though for the heart to live is the aim

I saw God stoop down one day

Caught me as by my hand

Cried on my shoulder, visited a Catholic's confession

Just from war in this land

He said, "Of all the prophets, ministers, rabbi's and priest

Churches organized for years

What's wrong with man? Why war? Ignore me?

Just to conquer your fears

There are other ways when your heart is right

To insure human just causes

But it takes restraint, honor for all human concern

Not hesitation from strategic pauses

To respect other people, their system or ideas

As you desire for yourself

Don't accuse them as evil or a constant threat

Because to you their beliefs are left

Better still, why don't strong countries, the big bosses

Stop selling lethal materials

If small countries want to fight – give free country

Let them develop their own theories

Such action is like the little kid brother

Depending upon a big brother to fight

He's always quiet when all alone but with his brother

In any collar he will light

I'm talking about America, powers of Western Europe

Profiting from lives at stake

The power of Russia that never fights

Finances those whose land she takes

This is where the UN could really give relief
Discuss this with powers she represents
When it comes to killing, underdeveloped
countries should be on their own
But for peace all resources are sent"
I discussed with God attitudes of employees,
labor unions and makers of steel
Those who profit from milk to leather goods
From a war whose nature is to kill
God what about the boost to the economy
Nature's way of population balances
God this is debate prevalent for a long time
Not to mention opportunities for selfish philanders
What about the opportunity to see the whole world?
Poor people couldn't do that before
This is the best time to see how foreigners live
My finances would have closed the door
In capitalistic countries money must circulate
To keep economies alive
Though in a war, unfortunates must die
At least somebody's wealth extends to the skies
Even further God, what would countries be like?
If Russia ignores the UN's plea
To not sell countries guns, ammunition or rockets
Fighter planes or ships that sail the seas
What if Russia continues to teach?
That freedom must be channeled through force
That to deal with democracy, as American history states
Is always a bloody course
Lord I'm just a minister, a chaplain for these men

Black but no less concerned

Than the chaplain who is a minister by your own *Call*

Seeking that we may discern

A black chaplain burdened by a strange paradox

Of black soldiers who raise possibilities

Of fighting the same way when returning to America

And denied inalienable liberties

Lord what do I do, stay in the military as a chaplain

Or try to beat these men back to the streets

To work in civilian churches, find relevant community action

Before a Civil War is a repeat

I don't anticipate who will win; the group

or race shouldn't be high priority

But to prevent unnecessary bloodshed; loss of hard-earned property

This is the hope of the majority

Don't get me wrong Lord; I'm black as any man

From anger of the soul and heart

I never have been or never will be

An Uncle Tom who only acts for his part

"I've been buked and scorned" just like those of my race

Just because of who I am

But you gave me a humanity that no man could penetrate

At telling me, "You're not worth *Uncle Sam*"

My mother worked and still works now for the lowest salary

Because of traditional society

We lived on the low economic ebb

Pressured by those professing Christian piety

So, Lord never place me among those of unethical schemes

Whether black, white or Jew

The only difference between me and the most radical militant

Am I'm trying to be like you?
So back to the war Lord, Oh I've seen how you act
You give men the freedom of choice
In every country, even other religious strands
You've never silenced your voice
Is it up to man? I mean action only through us
That's capable of producing peace?
Is there no other way, even to rob us of freedom?
That others will let others be.
God spoke to me again: "Elvernice, peace is not that complex
Stop letting seculars lead the church
I ordained ministers as leaders, spiritual values are too involved
Only good ministers have the touch
My laymen are to put my great sermons to work
In their lives, administrations or their vocations
When men aspire to know what God is like
Christians' lives ought to reveal information
International strife is only another arm of places
My Gospel ought to reach
But it must start at home and then spread abroad
The Gospel of love to teach
My Holy Spirit is with you always, encouraging, enlightening
That you may see the way
Though you have corporations, unions, cabinet members
The individual must accept me today
I won't take man's freedom to choose his destiny
Just place life for him to see
It's up to him, destinations depend upon him
America, Vietnam, for any liberty
I set before man death and life; sent prophets, even my Son

They said, "I am He!"
In war and strife, utter death, my hope – young man
May each let peace be
There is no excuse for man to act *ill rational*
As though he took my place
Throughout all history, all intelligence dictates
That man is only saved by grace
A grace that is amazing, powerful, and mysterious
From depths of Hades releases one's soul
A grace that can change you, make you stand upright
Regardless of your former goal
This I hope men will freely accept,
Withdraw from present evil conditions
Let them rise in the North, South, and any direction
And say, "I'm glad I've got religion!"
And then God looked away, closed his conversation
Looked as if disgusted with man
Then I said a prayer, because I know God cares
A prayer that America will take a stand

The next poem you are about to hear, like my first poem, was also inspired months after the TET II offensive where the North Vietnam leaders struck our forces with an intensive, all-out battle strategy to bring South Vietnam under psychological domination. TET like intensities continued until America pulled out of Vietnam under President Richard Nixon. Unlike the first poem, this poem developed over months, January – April 1969. During that intensity, history demonstrates that our soldiers continuously responded valiantly throughout each battle site.

However, the black soldier always had another battle to fight – the psychological war against what is identified as racism. I don't know which experience captivated the author the most at the time of this writing: the Civil Rights Movement still going on in the USA; counseling young soldiers affected by overt racial acts inflicted by their commanding officers and non-commissioned officers; watching black soldiers fight and die from battle in the midst of racial insensitivity; suffering the indignities of little things such as lack of needed Black products in the Post Exchange; the predominance of white girly sex magazines of which blacks were lynched in the US for pursuing their imposed sexual desires; and on the other hand giving the Vietnamese soldiers, both North and South, a sexual hunger for exploited, touched up brilliantly colored white female bodies; used for capital gains and to support white supremacy … (Please read preface to Poem 1)

"LET AMERICA BE"

Written in Pleiku Vietnam, January-April 1969
Chaplain (CPT) Elvernice Davis
Assistant 4th Infantry Division Chaplain
(All copyright privileges reserved by author)

What is a man's race that there should be such confusion?
And even "democratic" citizens fear thoughts of social infusion
When all present dreams of peace can only be an illusion
Because traditional methods of understandings
will intensify socio-nuclear fusions
And too, what is a nation, without meaningful consecration
Of the dreams and high principles
Established at its confirmation
Dreams of a free land, equal opportunity to every man,
To every woman boy and girl
From as many as every land
Why does it have to be that Communist always seductively smile
Whenever racially segregated congregations
In processions march down church isles

And the savior they try to persuade

Is said victorious over the grave

But on Sunday or church day mornings

They close their doors in some *God seeking* face

Why is it that families who found cause for their marriages to be?

Simply walk out or cause the other harm

Destroying the happiness of eternity

And the children, God bless them

Find before their life began

The unjust plights, the selfish deeds

Destroying the world's most powerful hand

Why should the value of one man, depend

upon the status of another?

Knowing that as even history proves

In this a man will kill his brother

And hence the reasons to still and kill

Or pay thousands for the mentally ill

The alternative though better is then concealed

Which is better than death, the right to live

Why should we make a bad example for countries that look up to us?

A nation so strong, so great, so bold

The motto of its wealth, "In God we trust"

Once a child, woman or man may find

And then in assistance we say, "Take without a pause"

They debate our intervention for their just cause

Why is it that the young is killed before their life began?

The hopes that grow dimmer, the dreams incomplete

Just because they needed that man

The young, the tender, the kind, the brave

Dreaming while lying in bed

The preventions of wars, or even their cause

And to end the diseases they dread

I've known some hippies and feeble gypsies

who were before pretense

As fine as any society knew

Until society stopped making sense

The classes they once so eagerly sought

To make the highest grade

The propositions embedded were robbed of truth

That tell how the country was made

They found some scholars and even their teachers

twisting truth without hesitation

As though the students who listen to them

Were without any estimation

Some of the students would just never mix

With those on the opposite sides of the track

But the majority of the young, making America strong

Just didn't dislike because faces were black

I have watched men of many a race, give

their all for America's beliefs

But only some will return to their land to suffer inhuman grief

Go back to Alabama, Mississippi, and the Carolinas

And see those he helped to save

"Can't serve you here, sorry not this job

We don't want your black face

And then come the burnings, lootings and

killings, just like ole Vietnam

The voice cries out with the tenderest plea

That's not like Uncle Sam

This is our nation, we only should fight

Wars for freedom on foreign shores

But in our own country, don't be distressed

One day we will open our doors

It's just not enough to make a report on

problems that start insurrections

Without efforts of government and all its citizens

Volunteering adequate corrections

This is certainly not a poem to support

That war is freedom's friend

I only warn and historically affirm

Frustrations never lead to choice ends

The high systems of education, the great resources we cherish

The beautiful homes in each community

Why should they perish?

Why highways and streets should be subjected to every danger

The beautiful parks, the exciting beaches

Tormented because of anger

The very young girl or even a young boy seduced by some maniac

The crippled old lady, some unfortunate widower

Never exempt from criminal attack

The poor, the rich, the black, the white

Never free to live on their own

They travel by taxi or in the company of friends

But hardly dare to go alone

Let's take a movie but when we stop to eat,

I wonder where policemen are

I heard on television and read in the paper

Just one block may be too far

Some guy with a family just off a farm

Desperately looked for a job

But due to no skill and/or the color of his skin

Nobody would give him a start

In the community where he lives, tragically,

minorities are like a hornet's nest

They must peddle dope or push prostitution

Whatever for them is best

Some play sports or they are called by the draft

To escape some of the misery

But too many remains victims of mankind

With no image of what to be

Don't keep telling the same old story, "Let

them make it like others before"

Except for fighting Indians, America was free

And the majority didn't close the door

I know along with the Indians, we fought the

British in the Revolutionary War

But, so did the African American before he was free-

Took part in every flaw

I want to see a country; the greatest I know

fulfill the dream of Martin Luther king

Not because he was African American or martyr for the right

But just to have freedom seen

To have the South or even the North see

What democratic is like

The voice of the people and I mean the people

Not the hero who put his finger in the dike

You know it's strange how people, just simple little people

Forget all the meaning or the sermons

Revealed on any church steeple

Of the one who was a Jew,

The world he came to save

This special kind of people,

How do we dare vision Christ's face?

The specialty is not confined to any ethnic groups

Not to race, economic status

Or even religious denominational troops

I speak to Christians who feel undebated responsible for one another

Who alternatively to Cain answer, "Yes!"

"We are the keeper of our brother!"

I can't believe the bad is more than the good and enslaves humanity

All it takes is the good to stand up and say

"All right, let them be!"

I've had friends' Lilly white and enemies

The colors of any night at dark

I learned early that skin is no trouble

If people desire the happiness of a lark

I know for some the word God gives them all the jitters

Except in severe wounds or sickness

When medics place them on litters

But name your God who must intervene

in social actions of our world

I'm sure your God would not condone the mistreating

Of any man, woman, boy or girl

The Bible speaks plainly: "Listen to me! You

atheist, you Christians, you Jews

Why should men of your intellect, your pride

Fear missing one day of any world news

Yet I know how you feel for there is no need to pretend

For the Achilles' heel of every nation

Is found in its weakness within
My record unveils the men made slaves, or
kings reigning on their thrones
Regardless of their battles or ultimate might
When neglect of me to death were prone
No philosophy or human zeal can fathom the total secrets of life
Every effort to find it or even create it
Without God always ends in strife
So, go on you friend and foe alike, let people be free to live
Just make sure you don't intervene
With the love they try to give
Just work on your own job, marry whom you please
But let others be perfectly free
People are too different, experiences to broad
For you to say who to meet
Why is it that others should decide, who should marry who?
From their divorce rate or marital problems
They didn't know what to do
Perhaps if they had been given society's freedom of choice
To marry whom, they please
Rather than wife swapping or dark road deceit
Their marriages could have been at ease
Then marriage is a part of a person's life
consecrated by divine consent
Outsiders who interfere can do more harm
Regardless of their intent
Parents should teach their children what
To look for when they marry
But when children reach adulthood remind them
"Remember, it should be a lifelong tarry!"

I'm sick and tired of America continuously play in her enemies' hand
And selfish politicians play on emotions
Rather than take a leader stand
I'm black and I've always been very proud
But this is my country too
A part of my heritage contributed to its greatness
No matter what people say or do
A shrewd enemy doesn't have to worry and
plot to win on a field of battle
Just trouble a man's home, his children, his wife
His ulcer is all that matters
Let him believe his future, his home is threatening to an end
Following his quarreling with neighbors
His enemy can more easily win
All my life I've never found differences because of a person's skin
The only philosophies I've seen developed
Stemmed from his country within
I haven't seen the difference in black or white men
Nor in black or white women either
And if it were not for problems of false orientation
There'd be no problems if neither
I've played with black and white boys since I was born
In a little Mississippi town
Played many children games with white girls too
Nobody in those days frowned
There were differences where we lived, certain
jobs for my father were not to let
But then we were equal again whenever
Anybody wanted to get in debt
Politicians should tell us; I mean those who preach segregation

As democracy's best friend
Most outrageous thing ever told today or before
The formation of intelligence did begin
The loss of the Civil War, wasted resources on
Separate but unequal schools
The revenue in taxes that could be paid by one
If he were trained to use the tools
I know how the rest of the nation frowns on Mississippi's plight
But there are other corners of our nation too
Who fear to come to the light?
We of any social status might was well confirm and agree
If the United States is to be any better
It must begin with me
Let me repeat I'm terribly concerned with problems tearing us apart
Because the problems we raise are more than disgrace
And never should have been from the start
I'm talking about conversations on downtown streets
People who could live peaceably together
We all know when we do what is right
It always makes us feel so much better
The joy on every street to speak to the stranger we meet
Springing from knowledge of the humility
When Jesus washed his disciples' feet
Hey, you miss, with the red dress on
And you man in the four-button suit
You drop out or you who follow orgies pad
There is a lot for you to do!
So, come on! Chin Up! Tell everybody you will make America Proud!
Say "I'm black, I'm white, I'm rich, and I'm poor"
Say it and say it loud!

Today may not reveal what a person is, or

What one day he may be

But if he doesn't start out facing every doubt

A failure he will go down in history

Get up all you young folks, old folks too!!

Let complacent call you mean!

Get off that comfortable pew or traditional excuse

Go out and do your thing!

You've got a contribution to make

A cause for which to serve

Your talent is the one that's unique

A gift only you can conserve

Come on!!

We've already got a man on the moon!!

Mars, the other planets

Who knows what's up there?

Stop sitting around fussing and fighting your neighbors

Everybody knows there's not a prepared heavenly stair

Get up!!

You are young, intelligent, handsome and beautiful!!

O Henry was wrong in saying

We are captains of our souls

But in another sense, he was right even to a Christian

What he does stems from strived at goals

Democracy can work if we give it a chance

Twentieth century mental cases

Aren't given up as lost

There are disorientations, people sick as raw sin

To get them well

Somebody must pay the cost

Confusion is an age old, negative, societal affair
Where men, though capable refuse launching into the deep
Primitive man fought each other
Segregated into tribes
To face the unchallenged
Some primitive should permanently sleep
I love democracy, the principles it entails, the red, the white, the blue
Because it's in freedom we can create
And even God makes old things new
Let student demonstrations, all social unrest,
end with our new president
All can be won if we give our consent
That our prayer for each other is meant

(All copyright privileges reserved by author, Elvernice Davis)

PIECING TOGETHER LIFE AFTER COMBAT EXPERIENCE

When the late Lieutenant General (LTG) Robert Grey, was Commander of the Signal Center and Fort Gordon, I served as his Command and Post Chaplain. I use his *public* phrase about "The soldier in the field." LTG Grey a highly decorated soldier, always gives the soldier in the field credit for his rank and the battlefield successes of the military.

I agree and must hasten to say, "Had it not been for the lower enlisted ranks, I would have never become the Colonel I became." I remember honest pre-dawn (the military term is "0 Dark Thirty") discussions of young draftees when in Vietnam we mustered to the perimeters from an alert of enemy movements and just downtime. I had opportunity to talk and listen to life stories. Some young white soldiers from the South would voluntarily talk about their being raised in Ku Klux Klan families and communities. They said that's the way it was. *"I was never taught to dislike and never thought bad about anybody or was not even around African Americans. Those I saw were on TV. Yet my mother always taught me to respect all people. Now I come in the Army and some of my best friends for life are African Americans I met in Basic Training and here in Vietnam. I can't go back to that."* Contrastingly, history is filled with the nasty, criminal facts of lynching, burnings while alive, unending travesties, of those the powerful sought to destroy.

During the Christmas break from war in 1969, I was assigned to do worship services and chaplain presence for a Battalion on stand down for a mop up after an extended B-52 bombing run. They were without an assigned chaplain. Relatives and American supporters of our soldiers had flooded the soldiers with Care Packages of small Christmas decorations, candies, cards and family pictures. Homesick already, the young soldiers, many their first Christmas away from home, deeply appreciated the efforts. Unaware of what they would face, I could feel their deeper feelings of dread for the imminent assignment of battle. The dread was well founded. Their mission encountered a well entrenched and trained enemy force and extremely high casualties. A few days earlier, we had laughs and talked, looked at pictures of girlfriends and spouses, listened to their future plans, sung Christmas carols, shared Holy Communion. For their country and families, many gave their lives and limbs and wounded bodies. Senior command members also shared the loss of life and severity of wounds.

Among downtime relationships there are some experiences inexplicably more troubling than others. After leaving Division Headquarters, I was assigned to 2/1 Calvary Squadron, headquartered at Blackhawk Fire Base on Highway 14 East. For 5 months, I had provided them chaplain coverage from Camp Enari, Pleiku.

Another deeply disturbing emotional crisis for me was once when leaving for chaplain supplies and coverage in our rear headquarters, hours before they were hit by heavy enemy attack. I loved my soldiers and I think they loved me back as their chaplain. *Chaplains have a "Mother Hen" type of protective feeling for their "flock."*

This was after spending two days bunking with and riding with

Commander C Troop, 2/1 Cav Squadron, on his *Command Armed Personnel Carrier.* His father was Four-Star Commanding General of Vietnam, General Creighton W. Abrams, Jr. Our mission was to search and destroy for a *North Vietnam Army (NVA)* Battalion size element.

Summoning a passing helicopter to take me back to the rear for repacking to visit another location of our command, and to bring hot food back to his command, I departed. Upon return, the pilot saw ground movement and that C Troop was surrounded by enemies waiting for the cover of dark. C Troop was, therefore, empowered to go on the offensive rather defensive. Still, very heavy casualties from death and wounds, the Commander was awarded the Silver Star in that battle.

The next day I returned for battlefield Memorial Services, counseling, chaplain presence and an unexplainable grief feeling for soldiers I had just visited. Having memorial services for deceased comrades with helmets draped over M16's, next to boots on the ground, is a memory hard to take for this chaplain and our soldiers in the field.

I stayed in Vietnam for one year when all I had to do was say "I no longer want to be a Chaplain" and could be discharged from the army in three days. I experienced our Division discharging a chaplain because of his stated position. I gladly stayed in Vietnam because of the soldiers in combat. I ended up spending 30 years in the Army Chaplaincy because I loved and felt committed to serve the soldier in uniform and his family for the good of a strong America.

Later in 1969, 2/1 Calvary Squadron moved south to open Highway 1 from Phan Rang to Phan Thiet. That first week we were inundated with monsoon rains. Later that monsoon rainy night, *while exhausted,* my Chaplain Assistant and I were awakened in our tent by a First Lieutenant from a Combat Engineering Company adjacent to our position. When I turned on the light, he seemed startled (*with flushed red face)* by me being black. He explained he had a black soldier that had threatened to shoot anybody that approached his shelter *half,* and he needed me to talk with him before we are forced to kill him. Sure, as I thought of my death from friendly fire. There was a perceived uneasiness about the Lieutenant as we approached his compound and the soldier's position. He was asleep and arousing him, identifying myself as the Chaplain, he came out. Looking harmless, I told the Lieutenant I would take him back to my tent for counseling. I had to insist as the Lieutenant wanted to be a part of the session.

Back at my tent, the soldier said the "night before somebody placed a hanging noose on his shelter half. I am the only African American in our compound. Everybody denied it. I requested seeing the Captain (Commander) and the First Sergeant and Lieutenant denied my request. I wanted to tell him to tell the soldiers I didn't think it was funny. So, in formation, without permission I said I'll shoot anybody who comes to my space with a hanging noose! The Lieutenant called me a "troublemaker."

Angered by the Lieutenant's *obvious* lack of leadership, my Chaplain Assistant and I drove the soldier back to his tent, I privately went back to the Lieutenant to ask if he knew the history of hanging nooses for black people. He said," Chaplain the soldier is a troublemaker!" I responded, "As a Chaplain, if I were in his shoes, I'd say the same thing!" His face again flustered red. The next day I saw the soldier at the Loading Zone (LZ). He was being sent back to the rear as a troublemaker. A few days later when his Chaplain, who was white (my Basic Chaplain Training School classmate) came for a visit, I explained the situation to him. My regret was inability to follow-thru because of distance from headquarters and combat requirements. My fear was this case would not be properly addressed and such a heinous case would not properly counsel a misguided field commander.

Consequently, another black soldier would return to America with racial chips on his emotional shoulder. Today my hope is that after combat experiences with multiracial and multinational support of Americans and allies, this Lieutenant, unlike some present draft dodgers, now elected to our highest political offices, changed his philosophical and psychological outlook. If not, he is a pitiful person.

Yet, there was to be a similar battle that happened months after our squadron had moved to open Highway 1 from Phan Rang to Phan Thiet.

Again, I had stayed one to two days in the fire base of B Troop when a late after dark chopper was summoned for pickup to carry their chaplain to the rear for visit to another location. After hearing active commotion that same night in the Operations tent, I learned B Troop was hit by enemy sappers, catching our troops off guard. With landing zone (LZ) too hot to land, at first light I returned with the Squadron Commander to very heavy casualties of dead and wounded, only one enemy dead of an *estimated* 10-man enemy sapper attack.

More memorial services, ministry of presence to grieving troops, unexplainable guilt for having just left before the attack, and with added incidents throughout the year, I am not grief free even to this day. But what about our young and old soldiers? They would say in conversation (tongue in cheek), "Chaplain, perhaps you should stay with us or not come back for a visit." They stayed on location, many times with fear and trembling. But they stayed and fought and died. The only means to be available to our Squadron was mobility.

Squadron units were spread out to different locations. Headquarters, A Troop, B Troop, C Troop, D Troop. Tanks, Armored Personnel Carriers, helicopters. Tactical support was also to all other military combat units in our operations. "We were soldiers."

With D Troop airmobile, our Squadron Commander advised that I, like he, cover the squadron and provide him briefings on troop morale, provide religious support, observe command problems with supplies or emotional stress, and other human frailties; visits of hospital and stockade, if necessary, and always recommendations. Lots of travel. *Never imagine Commanders who are not human beings* and wonderful leaders of our military *and Americans. Commanders are concerned for all troops in their command. They also cried with those of us who live. And the same or next day, they must assign and lead their commands in battle.*

I thank God for the many young and older soldiers who died and were wounded, and those of us who still live to tell the story, and for our American flag to fly high. And we promise that their deaths will not have been in vain.

CONTRIBUTIONS OF AN ASSIGNMENT TO SOUTH KOREA 1971

25 months after serving a year in Vietnam and a refreshing tour of duty at Ft. Jackson, SC, I was assigned to South Korea. Many of my Chaplain classmates were reassigned to second tours in Vietnam. I felt very blessed, not because I would have resisted returning to Vietnam (that was my rationale for becoming an Army Chaplain), but because the social pressures on my wife and parental family would be reduced.

In Vietnam, after the TET Offensive in 1968-69, my younger brother and I were in Vietnam at the same time. Bubble was of enlisted rank in the Air Force. Though the daily dangers he faced were not as catastrophic as mine from jungle search and destroy missions; combat head quartered in potential combat attack areas; traversing rice patties and jungled *and mountainous* areas for chaplain visits; with 2/1 Calvary Squadron or while being at the 4th Infantry division Headquarters and conducting troop worship or memorial services on firebases throughout the II Corps areas. Yet back home, Vietnam was Vietnam where, *in the minds of family members,* where no locations were exempt from direct human or rocket or mortar attacks. We are thankful that we returned home without Purple Hearts. Many close relatives, friends and other Americans paid the supreme sacrifices, and the wounded in mind and body still pay, for a war *many declare* as controversial at best.

In Korea, I was assigned with a senior Catholic Chaplain as Protestant Chaplain to the 20th Support Command Group, headquartered in Bupyeong west of Seoul. The Reception Station for all soldiers assigned to South Korea were reassigned out of this command. Also, the Army Stockade was located here for which I was also assigned as the Stockade Chaplain. This assignment would conjure within me racial frustrations that lurked below my conscious reality.

Don't misunderstand. Raised in Mississippi, as stated throughout this book, I was aware of racial inequities and problems. Yet I was raised in a family with an unusually strong father who both protected us from the terror and negative reinforcements of race and taught us racial and personal pride from a historical perspective.

At the same time, I was raised around American white people whose personal demeanor and practices defied the social negativisms commonplace to images of Mississippi. So, in terms of race, I could always see through the crux of skin color to the human condition. For example, my father always said: "Sonny a poor white man or a rich black man will make you kill them. Stay away from both!" *I regret his death before I explored with him the depth of his anger in saying kill rather than "Knock them crazy."* I knew he was not a racist and taught many positives about white people of which many were poor. *Among blacks he was respected as respectful of other families and extremely protective of his family.* Knowing the true intent was on protection of me, I spent a lifetime trying to dissect the rationale for this teaching.

There were fights in our Enlisted Clubs over Korean women. The fights on and off post were deemed as racial in our command staff meetings. I disagreed, that they were racial, and explained such fights over women occur in racially segregated schools, communities, colleges, even prior to military desegregation in 1948. I concluded that some men whether in restricted or diverse settings are just stupid. There was disagreement.

In a solicited private discussion for solution with our Commander, he said, "Chaplain, I can't help it if the Koreans just don't like black soldiers!" Instantly the images of my older brother George's discussion of his experience during the Korean War, and other black relatives and acquaintances who were soldiers during World War II, began to surface. They said for selfish reasons, Korean, French and German women, or women indigenous to their assigned areas, had been taught (as told by black soldiers) by white soldiers *to not date black soldiers,* because black soldiers had tails. Then, after experience, black soldiers explained how such women told them "how much they enjoyed their tails."

In my Chapel services was a faithful KATUSA (Korean) soldier. These soldiers trained with and partnered with American soldiers. Specialist 5th Class Kim (I have forgotten his first name) was very devout and a constant presence for private meditation and at all chapel programs. I decided to present him with the pressing question on race. My question and his answer began the professional, academic, building block for me on race.

First, surprisingly, Specialist Kim was 6 hours away from a Masters in Sociology at Yonsei University in Seoul. (Isn't God good?') He had, as told by him, completed translating Dr. Martin Luther King Jr.'s book "Why We Can't Wait" into Korean and was halfway through a translation of Charles V. Hamilton and Stokely Carmichael's book, "Black Power: *The Politics of Liberation.*"

Kim said immediately he felt a gush of inspiration and admiration for me he could not explain. The feeling was mutual. He *surprisingly, immediately* explained to me that the saying was a lie. "Koreans dislike all foreigners in their country and want their country back for themselves!" But rather than take his word for it, he requested that I let him design meetings with some local businessmen and businesswomen (prostitutes). He said, "No prostitute sees herself as a prostitute but a businesswoman," trying to make a living for her family. Then he said, I'd like for you to meet and discuss with Korean businessmen, businesswomen, students and professors at Yonsei University. See what they say, as I (received permission to not use names) but write the content of their conversations.

THE BUSINESSMEN

"Chaplain Davis, ten years ago, black soldier – number one, white soldier – number 10. Black soldier was always nice, made you feel good about yourself. White soldier treats you like dirt. Today, black soldier is very loud (Korean is a quiet culture), he wears long nappy hair when out of uniform; he comes in your store in groups so while you are waiting on his friends, they will steal your stuff; he treats Korean people very bad. Today black soldier is number 10. White soldier is number 10. White soldier thinks he is better than anybody in the world. We like his money but do not like the white soldier because he treats us like dirt. We do business because American soldier is the only way for us to make money to survive."

A good example is a Saturday I took to observe the Korean/US soldier culture. I took the military courtesy bus to Seoul for the day. The ride was free and the last bus to the post ran at, I think, 11pm from a selected drop off and pick up point. At an earlier stated return time, I and several soldiers were waiting, and the bus did not arrive. One of the American black soldiers invited the five of us soldiers to hire a taxi to take us to our post. He negotiated a price, told us our share and we were on the way home, stuffed in a small, compact Korean taxi. When almost there, the lead soldier would only collect from us half of our stated price. Once at the gate, he told the driver, "This is all you are getting. "You "Chinks always overcharge us black soldiers and you know it!" The driver said, "I told you the amount before we left Seoul!" He responded, "You take what I give you or nothing or I will kick your "Chink" ass all over this street!!" The driver, almost in tears kept asking for his money.

I pulled out my ID card as an officer and a Chaplain, then said to the group, "We all heard what the charges were and agreed. You are wrong and are misrepresenting ambassadors of the United States as ordered; now give the driver his charged fare. I added a tip and the soldiers knew best not to argue with me and left silently, probably cursing under their breath. Like career soldiers during Vietnam and especially commissioned officers, I perhaps was called a *"slur word!"* lifer and "Uncle Tom."

This was a period when the young American black was frustrated as to how to represent his American heritage. Ready to assert American black rights and pride, after duty hours which found them dressed in wide brim hats, loud colored clothing, bushy afro hair, playing loud music, traveling in groups and laughing and talking loudly. This was a radical contrast to the relaxed, quiet Korean culture and black soldier of the past years.

The military paper, "The Stars and Stripes" also complicated the problem by daily reporting the violent frustrations of the Civil Rights Movement going on in the USA. So, the young, usually drafted, Vietnam veteran or prospective combat soldier to be placed on orders to Vietnam, was angry at any confrontation that reminded of racial issues. Any "Lifer," (black, white senior enlisted, and any officer) were judged as having sold their souls to the system. Once I identified myself as an officer and a Chaplain, I immediately lost the respect of many of the emotionally and openly protesting soldiers, black or white.

Even senior white Sergeants reluctantly disciplined black soldiers were acting out, whether wearing hats in the dining hall or traveling in groups, knowing it pleased the soldier to be noticed in his protest. The accusation of being brought up on charges for racial reasons was a frustration for the entire command dedicated by tradition to maintain "Good order and discipline." It was a very tense social time, especially in theaters overseas. The following are additional summarized responses from the identified consults recommended by Specialist Fifth Class Kim, recorded by me *after and doing* the interviews.

BUSINESSWOMEN

"Chaplain Davis, Korea is a poor country! We were once occupied by the Japanese who treated us very badly. We still "deplore" all Japanese. Our parents are getting old. America has Social Security and retirement. We have no jobs, no retirement, except what the military gives us. Korea has no protection for old people. If I work on the base, the Army pays me very little money. I can make in one night what it takes more than a month for me to make on post and some soldiers want you to do it for free (have sex) or get fired. So, I save my money to buy my parents a home and one day I hope to marry a Korean man and have Korean children. I don't see race. I try not to feel soldier in my body who gives me money. White soldiers try to control territories and they pay well. If you go with black soldier, white soldiers boycott you and you lose much business. Black soldiers have their territory. Many don't want to pay well. Some even say we should pay them to go with black man. We don't want no foreigner but must make money for our family. Black and white soldier – number 10."

STUDENTS AND PROFESSORS AT YONSEI UNIVERSITY

I made one Saturday's visit to the campus and the next week I went home on Emergency Leave and was subsequently reassigned to Fort Hood, Texas. The students were not as vocal as the Businesswomen and Businessmen but also denied negative feelings toward African Americans.

I am very thankful for the subsequent compassionate reassignment to America due to family issues. Yet I also felt motivated to seek a truth that was meaningful for the contradictions discussed by African American soldiers from World War II and Korea. I believe God was in the action of having my return home for providential reasons. My younger brother had expressed security concerns for my revelation to him of my findings. In retrospect, I had, *including Vietnam,* initially under military orders, entered an anti-establishment research with very emotionally charged possibilities. The consequence was *the "tilt of an emotionally charged iceberg, for a professionally unprepared chaplain.* To God be the glory!!

Another job for me at **Bupyeong** *was that of being the Stockade Chaplain. On any given day, seemingly, a greater majority of the inmates were black. However, at least 90 percent of the guards and the Stockade Commander were white. In the stockade, among prisoners/guard relationships you could cut racial tension with a knife. The hostility of black soldiers toward stockade staff was horrendous. Without any training in Clinical Pastoral Education or Psychotherapy, I used every insight from seminary and 15 months "in the streets" of Chicago, between high school graduation and college, to forge rationale for effective conversation with inmates. After a month, it finally hit me that I was ineffective, and was on a different mental tract from the black inmates. All my intellectual strategies were oriented in Western thought. And I was working in a stockade that was managed by Western thoughts. I was* *a good theological student in seminary. But Karl Barth, Emil Brunner and Paul Tillich, et al were Western theologians. Rogerian counseling techniques nor Freudian concepts in psychology gave me much help. These black soldiers, draftees and volunteers, were schooled in Elijah Muhammad's "Message to the Black Man;" H. Rap Brown's racially slurred conversations and writings; Eldridge Cleaver's "Soul on Ice;" Richard Wright's "The Outsider;" and others. I decided that I, though also black, was scholastically and culturally unbalanced and irrelevant to enter their thought processes.*

With these frustrations a reality, I decided to dedicate myself to begin strategic reading each night. For the first six months, I would read only black materials that focus on the black problem in America. The next five months I would only concentrate on white materials that addressed the black problem in America. The remainder of time I would form a synthesis to construct an informed, personal position on the black problem in America.

All began to fall in place. Then overnight seemingly, I began to have meaningful counseling sessions with black inmates. I felt refreshed in pastoral ministry to all the troops. My input to the Command seemed more resourceful and appreciated.

And then, "whump!!" I was on Emergency leave after 6 months in country and compassionately reassigned to fort Hood, Texas without even the opportunity to say goodbye.

Little did I realize that intellectually and emotionally, I had become extremely negatively sensitive to racial differences for the first time. I was a racist, an ordained racist. This book will reveal how I was able to change my painful and bias racist outlook, to forge an understanding of mutual trust for conversation to take place. The historical alternative was for opposites to angrily "pick up their marbles" and go home, with intention of returning the next day ready for a fight. The feelings tapped were so deep that I realized identity with the "historical opposites" the impossibility without the help of God.

I returned to South Korea 20 years later as a Full Colonel and Command Chaplain of the Combined Field Army (ROK) in Uijongbu, South Korea. The first thing I noticed was the barren mountains of 1971 which were now filled with budding tall trees. Comfortable cars and trucks, though a rush hour all the time, had replaced bicycles that once carried 200-pound hogs, drunk on rice wine, I was told, to the market. My Deputy Chaplain was a ROK Chaplain. The only such combined command in the military, I was tremendously honored and blessed. I conducted the General Protestant worship services, provided counseling to all military personnel and family members who requested such services on our post, and participated in joint military training exercises; played in monthly joint golf tournaments; visited churches and pastors and toured religious retreat centers.

Our world's largest United Methodist Church was then in Seoul, Korea with over 54,000 members. I led a Transactional Analysis (TA) workshop for 30-50 young adults at Yoido Full Gospel Church the largest Korean Church with then over 100,000 members, (in today's count over 800,000). The TA class was arranged by my Korean Director of Religious Education who was a member of this congregation. Today, I am told by a Korean pastor, the church is rated as 1 million members. At a National Prayer Breakfast while I was in Uijongbu, the pastor said he was looking for space to house all his members at one sitting. He explained the doubts expressed when he first built his present church on swamp land to now be surrounded by high rise office buildings. His message was "Dream Big."

Supplied by translator headphones, I rarely needed a translator at any services I attended there. The young adults in attendance of my workshop were mostly college students and spoke fluent English. The churches translated into English, French and German. If it seems as though I was very busy, and I was, but still did much shopping and touring throughout the country. My family of a wife and three children were not with me. It was another year of difficult separation but outstanding pastoral experiences.

As I had fallen in love with the Korean people and culture during my first tour, it multiplied on my second tour with great admiration for this people who had endured war and oppression in their country, and were now making obvious social, economic and religious progress. My Deputy Command Chaplain, Chaplain (MAJ) Park conducted a powerful Korean Protestant worship service in our shared chapel. A contract Catholic priest conducted Catholic Mass. As Senior Chaplain, I enjoyed a full year of effective Command Chaplain experience in an enviable position.

A "LIVE WIRE" BLACK CHAPLAIN
AT FORT HOOD TEXAS

After six months in South Korea in 1971-1972, the first tour in the preceding chapter, it was great to be home in America. Our four-year-old son, for whom I had returned to America was now seemingly beyond his twice and sometime three times per month seizures of very high fevers that started when I departed for Korea. He was only 3 months old when I had departed for Vietnam. Carrel was spending 3-4 days per month in Columbus, MS Air Force Base Hospital which depleted the energies of my wife who lived an hour away from the base in the small town of Calhoun City, MS.

Our now, one-year old daughter, was the delight of her father's eye and Carrel was healthy again. We had bought a new home and had a great assignment in the First Calvary Division at Fort Hood, TX. The one problem, for the first time in my life I was now negatively, racially sensitive. Six months of studying racially sensitive stockade and command tensions; studying and experiencing racial issues in Vietnam, heavily induced in academic racial theory, and steady racial bombardment of Civil Rights projections in America, plus every day

American life, had unconsciously placed me in the positions of many white or black people who do not let themselves be human without enslavement to a political myth of racial superiority or inferiority. My wife brought it up many times, that I had changed, which I did not comprehend nor want to admit.

God did not call me into racial ministry. I was called into ministry. Now I found myself uncomfortable with weddings and baptisms for white soldiers. I did not want to feel patronized. Before Vietnam, ministry across racial lines was felt as normal. Now it was special with me, unprofessionally, and unnecessarily reminding the soldier or family that if they wanted another Chaplain, it was their right. They in turn would say "Chaplain, we came to you because we wanted you!" Praise God for his grace.

During this same period, while home, a sudden loud commotion brought Carrel and his three white friends to the front door. All were in the four-year-old range. One was screaming, Carrel holding a bat with wide bucked eyes, the other two were screaming "it's not his fault Mr. Davis!!" "Carrel, with frozen terror in his eyes, "what's wrong here?" I asked. The screaming kid said: "He hit me in the head with this baseball bat!!!!" I asked, fearful that the kid was injured, "why did you do that Carrel?" The two other kids shouted: *He called Carrel a "racial slur" word!!!! It's not his fault!!!* After examination, I determined the Emergency Room was not necessary and asked if he was all right and his reply was yes. I then asked if they could go back and play together, which they all said yes and did until families were reassigned. I watched them play for a while awhile to be certain his friend was not severely injured, Thank God! The social atmosphere was quiet again, after being disturbed by racial stupidity.

Carrel had done what his paternal grandfather had done in Vaiden, Mississippi approximately 59 years earlier at 25 years of age. *Daddy*

40

said a fellow white employee called him *a "racial slur"* and a fight ensued. White Masonic members had to slip our dad out of town. But subsequently, in his absence, *our mother described angry white men came to our home that evening,* his mother was hit in the head with a gun as she stooped to pick me from the floor. In all the mayhem, at 6 months I had come crawling and crying across the floor. I am told she was never the same again. Years later in Re-Decision therapy I learned that she nor I was ever the same again.

I pray God has forgiven me and the memory of any soldier who felt my frustration, and now I have been cleansed by God's grace. To my professional embarrassment, they would always say: "Chaplain we chose you, for our baptism and marriage or counseling, because we wanted you to do it! We feel great about you being our Chaplain!!" What a purifying blessing for me. Such a catharsis, though unaware of my theological pain, yet a purging of guilt that only they could offer.

Various situations occurred at fort Hood, and I was contemplating leaving the Christian ministry before one day I finally said: "OK Lord, I have a problem and I need you to fix me!" One day I had asked a member of my chapel services, a white Chief Warrant Officer, if he would have lunch with me. In the conversation, I asked if our services, though growing in attendance, would be more successful if I were white? He said Chaplain, "I don't know. Me and my wife and three teen age kids visited on your first Sunday, talked about it at dinner and all agreed that your sermon was powerful, and you are a great person. We look forward to coming every Sunday. You know, we never mentioned you are black!!!"

("It's me, it's me, it's me O Lord, standing in the need of prayer. It's not the preacher, nor the deacon, nor my mother nor my father; not my sister nor my brother, but it's me O Lord, standing in the need of prayer!!!") Convincingly for me it was, "Lord, I have a serious problem!! I need help!!!"

And just like that: the very next day my Division Chaplain, the late Chaplain (COL) Don Ude, called to say he wanted me to go to a spiritual retreat with Faith at Work, Inc. in Overland Park, KS. My first inclination was to say if this is going to be with some "white" group, I do not want to go. But it was being held in Kansas at a TWA Cabin Attendant training facility; the same week my *military* unit would be in the blistering hot training field with chiggers, mosquitoes, flies and dust. So, it was not the time to act "stupid."

Consequently, self predictably, here I was in a very comfortable remote setting, *in Overland Park, Kansas*, as the only black person among 17 whites trying to make sense of the Gospel through relational tools of people, psychological insight, the Holy Spirit and the Word of God. Dr. Karl Olson, *author of "Come to the Party"* and Group Leader of Faith at Work, Inc. was a Godsend, as well as my adopted family members. We adopted each other into our spiritual family. However, the adoption was only *a second day or more old* when I had an angry encounter with fellow family member, Lois, who called me a phony. *I was not sharing anything personally about me. "You are letting all us good white folks spill our poisonous guts while you are so clean, and sit there, listening with a smile!"* The next days and nights gave opportunity in group and private walks to begin socially to vomit raw, social poison spewed into our hearts and minds by an unsuspecting society. Poison that only grace and the power of the Holy Spirit could flush out of one's soul. In retrospect I can see I was always on the verge of explosion for the least perceived racial prompts. (God, I thank you for the so many angels you placed in my pathway for healing.)

Before I left Fort Hood a year or less later, God further used a member of my racially mixed congregation, a white nurse, who unknowingly gave me a tight, unwanted hug each Sunday with a "Thank you pastor, I needed that sermon!!" I would strategize while in the pulpit, *on* how to ask her to not hug me. I found myself wishing she would not come to worship in "My Chapel" not "God's Chapel." In her hugging me I deeply wondered what would her husband think? other white members of the congregation? The congregation kept growing and her husband, another Chief Warrant Officer in my command started coming. Unknowingly it was Ruth Boshee that God used to ultimately "hug the racial anger out of her pastor. Hallelujah and praise God for Ruth!" Thanks be to God thru Jesus Christ and the faith of Ruth Boshee!!! Teaching point? When in need and for the asking, God will send human "angels "… all whose knees have not bowed to Baal, and whose mouths have not kissed him." *(I Kings 19:18, KJV)*

During this same time at Fort Hood, my newly assigned Division Chaplain (COL) Conrad Walker had also selected me to attend a Clinical Pastoral Orientation Course (CPE) at the Presidio of San Francisco, CA. The late Chaplain Walker and his wife Ann would become a career mentor and lifelong friends. While at the Presidio I was, again ready for blows with a white chaplain (again I was the only black chaplain in my study group) for saying "I don't know who this guy is!!" He says he is Elvernice Davis; he wants us to call him "Dave; he has that ("cursing word") bracelet on his wrist that says "Sonny;" I think he is a phony and doesn't know who in *("cursing word")* creation he is or even thinks he is!!!"

Perhaps it was because the bracelet was a recent gift with my inscribed family nickname of "Sonny" from my baby sister thanking me for assisting her as a young sibling. Perhaps the combined frustrations of the Civil Rights Movement, Vietnam and Korea had finally knotted my *inability* to cope. For whatever emotional reason, I did not want white chaplains calling me Sonny. In my Basic Chaplain course, the white chaplains had asked to call me Dave rather than the long hard name of Elvernice. I accepted. Anything but Sonny.

Perhaps hearing my chaplain classmate classify my special gift as a ("cursing word") "insignificant bracelet" enacted a spontaneous combustion of rage and anger, out of character for the real me. I responded: "*I am whoever I decide who or what I want to be!!*" and stood up ready to go physical. The class was over. I went to my room enraged. On the TV was Sammy Davis, Jr. singing: "*Whether I'm right; or whether I'm wrong; whether I find a place in this world or just don't belong; I've gotta be me; I've gotta be me; what else can I be but what I am?*"

I said "that's who I am! That's where the music is. I am not Reverend Davis. I am not Chaplain Davis. I am not Dave! Even if I become General or Doctor, I am always Sonny!! I am Sonny of my parents, siblings, grandparents, family friends, church members. I was Sonny when I was called into ministry. I am proud to be Sonny!!"

I went back the next morning and apologized to the chaplain and group. (I don't remember the name of the chaplain or other chaplains in the group). The late Chaplain (COL) Cliff Weathers was the CPE Supervisor, and a Teaching Member from Eric Berne's Transactional Analysis School of Psychotherapy in San Francisco was a resource teacher. While studying on the Presidio Army post, a female member of the group invited me to attend Glide Memorial UMC and I remember an encouraging sermon by Pastor Cecil Williams, although having created a cutting-edge ministry with "Street People" in San Francisco. Cecil later became the go-between contact between the San Francisco political authorities and Patty Hearts and the SLA anti-establishment group.

Except seeking references in TA for dealing with racial issues, I remember nothing else except hospital visitations at the Presidio. The experience there was a critical medical catharsis for this Vietnam chaplain.

From that instance, I became "Sonny" for the rest of my military career. I didn't have to compete for it, be ordained for it or be rewarded for it, nor could it be taken away. I was me. I would always be "Sonny" who happen to be whatever was to be achieved. I was free to be me!! Thanks Sammy Davis, Jr!!! And the rest of you!!! God placed you in my life, even you who provoked racial anger, and you didn't even know it! My beloved Army career uncle was also named "Sammy Davis, Jr. - I always exclaim, "The poor one." But he nor we were poor. I've seen too many poor people. We were not and are not poor.

From Fort Hood after three years, I was assigned to the eleven months Career Course of the US Army Chaplain Center and School, and was invited by the Office of the Chief of Chaplains to study for an additional fifteen months at Southeast Institute of Psychotherapy in Chapel Hill, NC for a Post-Graduate Fellows in Psychotherapy. I had just graduated from the *11-month Career Chaplains Advanced* Course and Long Island University in New York with a Masters in Sociology. For my professional paper, I researched racism as confined in words of songs of the Armed Forces Hymnal that, perhaps, unconsciously precipitated social division in communities rather than Christian unity.

This study was precipitated from a morning chapel worship service where we were invited to sing a hymn with words: "My soul was black as sin." In spontaneous silence I raised the "Black Power" fist of Olympians Tommie Smith and John Carlos. Yes, back in our small group, I reiterated my feelings. Some of my classmates were understandably negative and angered by such a thought and action because these hymns were and are used widely in many church services today. *My one black classmate agreed privately but said nothing in the group.* One fellow white chaplain said, "If I have to change my language just to relate, I don't want to be a chaplain for black families." From Georgia, he could not grasp the internal rage among African

Americans elicited for decades by *Senator Strom Thurmond with enraged enunciation of reference to African Americans,* in referring to black people; Governor Lester Maddox of Georgia with his axe handle; neighboring Governor George Wallace of Alabama and a historical host of other historical and contemporary so-called racial segregationists, as rabid as historical Governor James K. Vardaman of Mississippi.

Rather than change, my chaplain classmate saw language not as a tool to be adapted to fit communication of necessity for the sake of spreading the Gospel of our Lord. So, I intimated that if he followed his embedded threat, he would not advance the kingdom of our Lord but assist the work of racial division empowered by Satan. This Chaplain was not a bad person but like many of his community (neighborhood), was only practicing what they have been taught by threat of severe social ostracism or even death.

My chosen task and opportunity given by our Army Chaplaincy at Southeast Institute was to gain an understanding of racism from a psychotherapeutic perspective, using the tools of Eric Berne's Transactional Analysis out of the Gestalt orientation taught by German Psychologist/Psychiatrist Friedrich Salomon Perls or Frizs Perls.

While still seeking, common sense and researched rationale for a myth, I contend, causing most of the world's social harm, President Graham Barnes and Vice President Josephine Lewis had brought a workshop on Racism to Fort Hood which deeply inspired me as an attendant. The assigned workshop had providentially coincided with my return from Clinical Pastoral Education training at The Presidio Army Base in San Francisco. God was answering prayers of the faithful. After the workshop, Graham invited me to study at his Chapel Hill, NC Institute of Psychotherapy which he had founded after seeing America's cities burning following the assassination of Dr. King. Graham said, "Something has to be done" and this was his something as an ordained minister of the Church of Christ. I had placed in my military file a request to the Chief of Chaplains to attend his Institute.

Providentially, I was taken off orders to Germany and given the opportunity for enrollment for a year of civilian schooling which ended with fifteen months of study at Southeast Institute with additional Vice President and TA Teaching, Member, Reverend Dr. Vann Joines. I am thankful to God for being one of two chaplains in my class, chosen from our Army Chaplains Advance Course for back to back schooling. I am always indebted to God and our senior military chaplain leadership for this great honor.

I learned much and used the insights widely throughout the remainder of my chaplain experiences and military ministry until this day, yet there is still so much work to be done. Perhaps in some way, *this book is payback for the faith and sacrifice for God to use me through the wisdom of chaplain supervisors.*

Throughout this book the book theme of former Secretary of State and Presidential Candidate Hillary Clinton resonates with "It Takes a Village!! I am village made.

If you only said: "Good morning!" to me with a smile, you made my day. If in bitterness or suspected criminal intent of two young men, as I explained to a policeman while shopping at Walmart in Memphis, they made me quote Graham Barnes in saying "Something has to be done!"

THE INTENT OF THIS BOOK

The intent of this book is not insistent upon eradicating the Christian Church as an institution from an acclaimed Democratic and Christian society. During the 60's, this was a cry of some Civil Rights reformers. Neither do I believe that to reform a political or social establishment is futile without first destroying or completely disruption of the context of its foundation. *I believe wars between people and nations have such conclusions knitted into their justification.*

I do not believe that of necessity older persons, who also were once young, must be physically consumed prior to the construction of just and virtuous institutions. The saying "one cannot teach an old dog new tricks" should not be relative to human beings. Lower orders of nature act primarily on instincts. Human reactions are conditioned by at least three responses: instinctive, emotional and rational.

This is not to overlook the perennial phrase: "Once a man; twice a child." Whereas Socrates was convicted for poisoning the minds of the youth, perhaps those who intentionally confuse and poison the minds of senior citizens, in whatever form, should also face the gallows.

I have seen persons, those of most illicit moral conduct, respond to the call of God as ministers, dedicated laymen or make radical personality changes in their middle ages or older ages in life. I regret William Barnes of Christ United Methodist Church, Memphis, is deceased before hearing me quote his approved example to me. Barnes said to me: *"In his younger years he was a racist. The people around him were racist. That's all he knew. But the Lord and study changed his life so that, at 85, he did not have a racist bone in his body."* He lived by his political convictions of Party affiliation, but "his Party did not always reflect the religions convictions of his soul."

I have seen local churches, without any degree of relevance in its community. Yet I have seen those churches spring to life prior to additional equipment, at the presence of new leadership. The equipment already possessed was intact. It was not the fault of the equipment but the indifference or capability of those whose responsibility it was to make the inanimate alive or to place concreteness on abstract principles.

I do not believe the "generation gap" today is the results of philosophical irrelevance so much as a lax attitude toward perfectly useful philosophical or religious principles on the part of older persons. The generation gap is a chasm between those who are comfortably complacent with admiring Utopia's and those whose determination is to transform Utopia into the grasp of their *reality*. There is a positive answer to the question, "What are the young folks up to?" Young people simply dare to live a life of honesty because they have experienced the resultant social sickness of hypocrisy and utter deceit. *Generationally, we should pray that the young will capitalize on their learnings for the sake of a socially healthy and changed future.*

Each generation has seen and experienced the personality damage to heredity or posterity resulting from a false perception of life. The young generation has learned that however powerful the mind may be, the decision is not that of the mind to determine the reality of a fact. The young are prone to recognize the inevitability of facts. Alterations and induced changes are prevalent in the fields of modern technological research. Contemporary findings necessitate theoretical revolution as the theories are proven false. But to have a choice in accepting a comfortable theory simultaneously with an unquestionable fact that evidently contradicts the given theory is simply highly ridiculous. Absurdity in the "youth movement" is primarily the consequence of naivete. Quite the contrary, absurdity in the "older generation" is essentially the product of honest hypocrisy.

I contest the ultimate value of racial group consolidation and deification. In an era when the earth is being transformed into a community, I do not argue that the black man or any race should know their heritage. I do not question that all people should pride in their ancestral tradition. However, to the Samaritan woman Jesus announced a change: *"...Woman, believe me, the hour cometh, when ye shall neither in this mountain, nor yet in Jerusalem, worship the Father ... God is a spirit, and they that worship him must worship him in spirit and in truth." (John 4:21,24., KJV)*

Debates are meaningless which preclude that African Americans should not be recognizing a rightful place in American and or World history. Especially in communities where the legal authorities will not protect the legal rights of the Americans of color, there is no alternative than for that community sector to take the law in their own hands. That too is a Constitutional right.

I do not believe that every person desirous of just treatment under American law should passively subject themselves as a martyr. This has never been a personal ultimate persuasion. As a participant in a non-violent demonstration, I was always ready to accept verbal or violent abuses without physical retaliation. Nevertheless, if the same actions had threatened the security of my family at home or on a casual shopping or leisure tour, my reactions would have been quite different.

The moral aim of non-violent demonstrations was to awake the moral consciousness of our nation with the minimum cost of human lives or in destruction of physical property. So called militants worldwide today have lost faith in the reliability of such movement in achieving their goal of freedom. Many have lost interest in racial integration even before the goal of human justice has been achieved. I do not favor racial integration for the sake of social infusion but for the sake of freedom. Racial integration for purely integration sake is a "whistle in the dark and was never the goal of the Civil Rights Movement.

There is no virtue in living next to a family just because they are white or black. There is no virtue in interracial marriage just because the other is black or white. The virtue lies in the freedom to be American in its ideal emphasis and that freedom of "life, liberty and the pursuit of happiness."

Black power, ultimately, must be a tool for the establishment of justice for all persons inclusive and exclusive of the black or white race under the *"Constitution of the United States of America."*. Black power in America must be focused on a justifiable end in a democracy rather than an end in itself. American citizens of color are wise to pool their resources to be independent of unjust exploitation. Howbeit, if business or independence is enslaved by merely racial isolation against contribution for the perfecting of the total society, that effort shall be degenerate in exercising its maximum potential. In addition, too much of the wealth of Americans of color and toil is already invested in modern conveniences to voluntarily accept starting anew with the little owned as a race. Since Americans bought prosperity for a price involuntarily or voluntarily paid for, all Americans should enjoy the "reaps of the harvest."

The contention of this book is that contemporarily, substantiating theories and beliefs about Christianity and Democracy, *as historically and* theologically documented today, may be enough for contemporary social chaos. Our United Methodist Church is threatening to split today over one issue, homosexuality. Once race was a splitting issue which is not yet perfected. Now here we go again. Our problem is not resource material. Our problem is not difficulty in understanding the "whys" of social frustrations.

One of Stokely Carmichael's strong points was that the Civil Rights Movement was not to teach Blacks their rights under our Constitution. The challenge was to teach whites that blacks had inalienable rights under our Constitution.

Except as a description in the English language, the identity of a black and white church is not biblical. It is a social phenomenon robbed of the power of the Holy Spirit commissioned at Pentecost. Either identity is a myth limited by the circumstances of neighborhood. The colorless, raceless and cultureless church is a community church whose identity is empowered by the Holy Spirit. Any modification to its structure, drains the power it could otherwise use for the glory of God's formula for his kingdom on earth. Perhaps if the theology of this type of churching could replace the contemporary racial way of theologically excusing churching in the 21st century, democracy would have a powerful existential ally to lead other world communities.

There are many definitions of church so I hold to the definition I learned in seminary which has stood the test of my discussions: "A church is a body of believers, called by God, and drawn into a fellowship, in order to worship, witness and work, in Christ's name, and that by the power of the Holy Spirit."

With everything else being considered, the problem is acting positively on the things we know are right and just. Social friction exists because somebody will not "treat others as they themselves desire to be treated." The problem of drug addiction, for example, which enhances criminal assaults and prostitution and suicide, is resultant from selfish, some otherwise respectable persons in the community, with a profit motive. What we need today is not new social legislation or a new Christianity. To live according to the guidance of the "old" will solve most of our present problems in interpersonal relationships. If communities will use the moral guidance, they already have, in dealing with their crisis, crises can become minimum.

I write because the American people of today, though not different from ancestors in temperament, will no longer remain passive. Passivity is a tactic and not a condition of nature. The "yas sir," "boss," and "massa" of yesterday were utterances of psychological interracial brainwashing upon white dominance for reasons of survival. Though massive revolts were constant threats to slave systems, blacks remained passive as they used wisdom in appraising their total outcome. History has not known a bravery, that surpasses the revolt of American black leaders whose people were mercilessly exploited and without voice, weapons, educational or political skill, yet were plotting ways of escape. Thank you, Harriett Tubman, and so many more!

There have been no greater love stories than couples in love who after giving birth to children were forced to the "slave blocks" to be sold like cattle to the highest bidder. It does not take imagination to realize the anguish, the terror, the emotional strain of persons, inherent depression whose depth of grief was unfathomable at prior knowledge of forced separation. Human intelligence of any oppressor, black or white, is without excuse to state, "my oppressed people love me."

The South, because of its agricultural necessity, has been a prevailing victim and perpetrator of its ancestral practices. Although many were constantly seizing the possessions of the poor or disenfranchised, which is a most spiritually degrading crime, as late as the twentieth first century, who could love those that take advantage of American citizens? Even taking possession of private real estate because owners could not afford the taxes before or levied after unjust re-appraisal, although legal, is just evil.

As I watched families of the Charleston, SC massacre and recently the 18-year-old black male who heard the judicial conviction of murder, hugged the white female murderer of his brother, with words on media: all said, "I forgive you!" In those instances, the context of racial insults cannot occur in the same expression. They are struggling with a psycho-physical principle of Jesus to forgive regardless of the crime although justice should be a preferred action of the courts. The issue is can one love before forgiving or is Tina Turner's *"What's love got to do with it?* a necessary discussion? We must love our aggressive neighbor? and forgive those who continuously trespass against us? Are these conditional responses or unconditional responses? You clarify such in Sunday School.

Many in the South during social unrest said these Northerners are down South stirring up trouble. This was another discount of the feelings and thinking of those oppressed for years because of disenfranchisement, unequal access to decent jobs, equal education, respect at the marketplace and decent housing. The American family of color has seen and experienced illegal lawsuits for generations. American black families have known the double standards of prices that made their American white families rich from condoned means. Still, many insensitive persons may claim, "I am loved and respected because they will do anything I ask!" No, it's because they try to follow Jesus while still fighting to get the unjust boot off their necks.

I remember interracial group discussions; remarks were intended informational that the American black and African black are different persons. The American black is not a man, they said, of pride whereas the African thinks highly of themselves and is themselves insulted to be called African American. There has never been a more incorrect statement. First, is a cultural difference. The American black developed under a pseudo environment and consequently found it rewarding to participate in a pseudo fashion for the best profit. Africans owned their continent until shrewd tactics; pseudo *acceptance, murder* and genocide were used to give foreigners a foothold. The difference, of course, being the American black citizen's pretense was for survival, his African counterpart for profit during American slavery, curiosity and social exploration.

This condition is primarily the cause for psychosomatic illness in race relations today. For centuries, the prevailing inhabitants of America accepted this pseudo concept of sociological differences when the truth was known. The oppressed black man smiled when his very soul cursed. The oppressor himself boosted his own ego as the American black pretended recognition for his superiority, knowing the person in conversation hardly considered what he said.

For me this was always a problem. Until in group therapy years later, I don't know when the vow was made, but I have always thought in the extreme in, not aggression, but in retaliatory violence against whites. This was not taught in my family of origin, my school or church, which dominated my conscious thinking. However, my promise had always been that if a white man ever kicked me, as was southern custom, at the first opportunity I would not stop short of murder. Many times, I thought I was close to making the decision, but God always intervened. I consciously used the "Pseudo Good Black" ("Sir, I Just didn't see the lady; and ignoring the man, "Maam, I just didn't see you getting out of your car and I'm sorry!). I was sweeping the street in front of the store and overlooked the lady getting out of her car. Showing southern custom, he walked up as to kick me and I stood waiting and willing to sacrifice double homicide, if I were kicked). Anger and revenge run very deep into the psychic of human beings. I will discuss Re-decision Therapy later in this book.

In community violence, I would always go to normal extremes to prevent trouble. Basically, as a Christian I wanted to live peacefully with everybody because of my father's involvement, partially because of my family but always because of (Romans 12:18, KJV): *"If it be possible, live peaceably with all men."* In the practices of civil violence against African American communities, past and contemporary threats in America make it seem impossible. My aim was always to prevent trouble but if conditions were forced, Jesus died to show us how-to live-in peace. I do not believe that martyrdom in facing the devil especially, is a requirement for every Christian believer.

Some African Americans accepted overt passivity as a minor tactic in the latter days of the quest for freedom under the leadership of Dr. King. However, the proliferation of assault weapons today fanatically mimics American history; that to achieve freedom in America is to inflict violence upon those who would challenge it for all Americans

Tacticians in pleading for social revolution, seemingly, are ready on all racial sides to ally themselves with whatever advantage is before them to achieve victory *in what they perceive as inalienable Civil War.* There is no longer the willingness to be insulted, dehumanized and denied what sweat and blood from war after war and required payment of taxes of all ethnic citizens have bought. There are many who take literally the idea of the African American Spiritual: as the Original Colonies before the Revolutionary War, "before I 'll be a slave, (Or before I accept a lesser social status) I'll be buried in my grave and go home to my Lord and be free." That is radical suicide.

The time has come, when Americans are denied human rights, adult temper tantrums are the properties of all human beings. And for incompetent and profit motive leaders who say, "let them try it then, we can do something about that;" the intelligent response is no, because Americans are again playing into the hands of those who seek to destroy, and as in all wars, both the aggressor and the aggressed will suffer catastrophic losses and destruction. *Religiously, I can imagine in the Rapture some person of divinity, looking over the world weeping the destruction, as Jesus when in (Luke 19:41, KJV), wept over Jerusalem. If in a hermeneutical discussion, I could hear Jesus saying today: "You crazy people! How did you think you could encourage a 21st century civil or world war, and believe you would be the only survivor?"*

American citizens interested in God and Country should support just and virtuous practices under a democratic system of orientation. Even if theory were the only reality, black or white power, without therapeutic convictions concerned only with justice, fair play and freedom for all concerned, is tragic. Black or white power should have a *universal or community* goal and that goal should not be vengeful or to oppress and destroy but to correct and build up. History is there, for those who respect it, to shine a bright light so that walking in darkness is not a repeat. The "Good ole days" were not good for the millions of people who were raped of bodies and lands, murdered by the unforeseeable types of death; impoverished, lynched, diseased, starved, should I go on?

Percentage wise, I believe there are a few, who without clear thinking, say "I lived in the good ole days" and in retrospect, while living in a police controlled society with strong white protection and control; sleeping in the beds they made which were sleepless nights, with consciousness not free of guilt; the fear of dying without their souls being saved, or from the hands of those who sought their possessions and spilled blood. Before George Orwell's Animal Farm, there were always the Animal Farms of American Indian wars, Civil War in America, era of Reconstruction, World Wars I and 2, Korea,

Vietnam - Okay, all the wars. *At five years of age I still remember our running into the house when low flying airplanes serving Camp McCain, MS flew over our homes. We feared the enemy was about to drop bombs. Children and adults in the 21st century yet experiencing real instances of this evil reality.* Though life and death, good and evil of Deuteronomy 30 were placed before Americans as choices, Americans have always had difficulty over choosing life or death and destruction. It was always death and destruction. When will we change?

What do I mean? The world must re-evaluate the value of blackness and whiteness. Black and white persons need to pride in their being *for which they had no control.* Black and white are beautiful. Yet neither are even the colors described. The physical color of a person does not complicate or create discriminating imperfections that are not common to any other people of different skin color. God given intelligence is potentially synonymous to that of white, black, or any given people. Therefore, when oppressors, for selfish gain, organize to discriminate or offend Americans based on group identity, the Christian church, representing Jesus as the only way to life and peace, knowing the truth (Does it know the truth?), should organize and rise up to defend posterity. The Constitution premises on Christian precepts.

In the United Methodist Church, of which I am a proud member, if a white caucus becomes determined to deprive other members of representation and voice in matters of inevitable racial effects in membership and policy, like bees in a beehive, unification of all members is necessary to defend its core. Yet caucusing becomes a human strategy to deal with the political imperfections of the whole body. This is especially true when mergers with other white memberships become priority and successful over against that of black membership whose historical mother churches fail in seeking the same restoration.

At the time of merger, a black Caucus formed Black Methodist for Church Renewal (BMCR) and a white Evangelical United Brethren church were merged to establish the United Methodist Church. BMCR succeeded in assisting elections of bishops, District Superintendents, representation of Directors and staff in national and Conference Commissions, etc. Yet at the local church level, membership of African and White American churches has drastically declined. This is true in most Liturgical churches to great disappointment. The primary causes have produced the writing of many books.

If our churches had merged at the Local Church levels on the identical percentages of at the higher office levels, I question whether the outcome of membership ultimately would have been different. We will never know. The impossibility hinged on the rigid separation of the races into neighborhoods. Whites and blacks have been systematically taught for centuries to be suspicious of each other. At the Conference or administrative level, under encouragement for acceptance by powerful and respected neighborhood leaders, District Superintendents, Bishops and some pastors were welcomed into communities regardless of race.

Nevertheless, when people examine themselves, they do not abhor each other because of race. Profiteers of race know that. That is my finding when I conducted and attended numerous Race Relations groups in Army settings. And when they, interracial groups, come together in peace or in Christ, *they have a jubilee time.*

In my home state of Mississippi, I believe in terms of racially interracial leadership among clergy and laity in the church, the Mississippi Conference is a model for other Conferences to imitate. Black power then, or white power, even in the Christian church, should be a social light used as a Pentecostal tool and to energize Christians coming together in community, rather than to racially segregate them in neighborhoods as heathens at the local level while racially integrating at the executive level. As United Methodists we may blame each other for our decline, yet blame is a high energy "temper tantrum" of 6-year-old kids" which in many cases only receive a spanking by mature parents who see their mistakes.

In a theological connotation, black power to me, as angry, at the past and present it is, (we are), of greater priority must concern itself with the universe, not the neighborhood of Jonah's day. It is the universals that enslave the neighborhoods.

The 21st century is filled with capital gain projections on rebuilding walls for gated communities and even between nations. Howbeit, to correct an ancestral European mistake in building the Berlin Wall, President Ronald Reagan became famous for calling out the General Secretary of the Communist Party of the Soviet Union: "Mr. (Mikhail) Gorbachev, tear down this wall!" The Presidential address was delivered in West Berlin on June 12, 1987. To prevent the repetitious, generational physical and social wall building and tearing down, the global community of Christian churches, like Joshua's strategy of marching around the walls of Jericho, (Joshua 6:1-27, KJV), must in the name of Jesus, "Tear down these walls!"

Power advocates would also be wise to visit a psychological teaching by Eric Berne, in his book:" What Do You Say, After You Say Hello?" Berne, agreeing with other psychologists, says when in anger one is never more than 6 years of age. Only six years of age to handle critical adult responsibilities. It is no surprise that God says to Zechariah: "Not by might, nor by power but by my spirit…" (Zechariah 4:6 KJV) Might and power are bullies at the neighborhood and community levels. Vann Joines of Southeast Institute (TA) describes a bully as a scary kid, walking around on stilts. If his stilts are taken away, he falls and cries like a baby. Any tool used as an opportunity for revenge carries along with it prolonged and the formation of a new, as of not yet, traditional problems.

As a senior in high school, I received a punishment I conceived to be unfair. Amid the deeply ingrained anguish toward the teacher, I promised myself that I would become a teacher and return to that school just to punish the teachers' children the same way (I did). It would have been unwise to retaliate against the teacher because he had the authority and I was guilty of the accusation.

In later years, I critically observed the teacher's son. A young man, likeable, intelligent and completely unaware of his father's actions toward me. Incidentally, the same son, associated with my younger brothers in attempting to re-establish rules that time had made obsolete. Had I taken a vengeful act, I would have possibly prolonged the valuable combination of talents that began to reshape policies, that I regrettably accepted, and the cooperation that can contribute more to the world than I, because after I am gone, logical progression could continue. This same son respected me so highly that he wrote a full-page article of me as an Army Chaplain and other accomplishments in the town newspaper. *Human creatures are not smart enough to play God.*

In this regard, as a black power or white power that divides, that fosters unlimited suspicion, that in its efforts to alleviate, picks up the rod of the oppressor, is dangerous even to itself. A power that aligns itself with color over against principle, which is repetitious of the history power resents, will prolong the patterns of that same history. Regardless of who a person happens to be, if their mind is of accord with the principles inherently virtuous and is willing to give of themselves to create identical goals, it is the person and not ancestral beginnings that's persuasive. Dr. King so eloquently quoted Ralph Waldo Emerson this way: *"Truth forever on the scaffold; wrong forever on the throne; Yet tis truth that sways the future and behind it all stands God in the dim unknown, keeping watch above his own."*

Black power, within itself, within the neighborhood, offers no alternative to the same trend. Under black power, blacks are fearful to associate with whites whether male or female. Above all, younger blacks once feared honorable jobs or higher academic grades, where they can perform useful tasks, because they were afraid of being labeled an "Uncle Tom." "Let freedom ring" may be hampered if black power does not restrict itself to achieving definable and justifiable goals within the context of the Christian faith and democracy. Under no circumstance, should it become guilty of ruling the lives of its constituents the same as its opponent seeks to rule the lives of its adherents by color, intimidation and or aggressed violence. Both miss the boat of freedom.

"TREES ARE FALLING"

Every plant that my Father did not Plant shall
be Rooted up. (Matthew 15:13, KJV)

I remember a sermon preached during the abolishment of the Central Jurisdiction of the Methodist Church to the Upper Mississippi Annual Conference of the Methodist Church, by Dr. Joseph Lowery. Dr. Lowery used (Matthew 15:13, KJV): "Every Tree that my Father did not plant will be rooted up." He titled his sermon, "Trees are Falling." As an example of plants, he focused on Egyptian slavery of the Jews, American slavery of Africans, Apartheid in South Africa, Jim Crowism and racial segregation in America. He emphasized these as plants not planted by God and would be rooted up.

I have not changed my focus on emphasizing that the primary problems of America are embedded in the failure of America as a nation to practice the tenants of religion it publicly adheres to.

When my deeper thoughts began to develop for this book, President John Kennedy was alive. Dr. Martin Luther King, Jr. had not been murdered. Senator Robert F. Kennedy was still alive. The Democratic Convention of Mayor Daley in Chicago was not foreseeable. The violent international rebelliousness of college and university students had not erupted. The report of the National Advisory Commission on Civil Discord of "Greenwich Villages" or Haight Asbury's" or anti-church sentiment was only on a normal incline. Grenada, Mississippi's violent demonstrations against school desegregation in Mississippi had not given the creation of the "Black Power" slogan. Students at the University of Mississippi had not filed a petition for the freedom to select speakers for the student body. Mississippi had no black congressmen nor black public officials.

There were no convictions of white persons who viciously murdered or attacked unarmed or non-violent African Americans in Mississippi. Malcolm X was increasing in power. The Black Panthers were hardly known. Adam Clayton Powell was chairman of the House Education and Labor Committee. Tom J. Altizer and Willian Hamilton had not yet popularized their presentation of a "hermeneutical" death of God theology. Their book "God is Dead," to me was a hermeneutical acknowledgement in the sense that even the "preacher" of the *biblical book of Ecclesiastes* had raised the same possibility of a world spinning on its own axis. The crisis of Catholicism as we know it today was less critical at the writing of this book.

I am of the opinion that, if the Christian church had ideally capitalized on the influence it possessed in America, at least the racial problems of today could have been minimized. It would have paid an enormous price, but we sang in our United Methodist Hymnal: *"Am I a soldier of the cross; a follower of the lamb; And should I fear to own his cause; or blush to speak his name? Must I be carried to the skies on flowery beds of ease; while other fought to win the prize and sailed thru bloody seas?* Should this hymn be banned from Christian worship?

I use the word church to include all religious denominations, whether black or white, that condoned the racially segregated and exploitative traditions of the American culture. I hope the martyrs and heroes who encouraged me and fought, and still fight, this degrading plight of the Christian church, will hear me acknowledge their and our struggles.

Our U.S. Constitution offers American churches all the power needed to implant Christian virtues in theology and civil law. An echo of the Constitution is "Free exercise of religion." Yet after the courts abolished racial segregation and inequality of education in public schools, many of our churches allowed secular thinkers to use our sacred spaces to legally re-segregate schools, churches and neighborhoods. Consequently, rather than citizens optimize learning to know and respect each other as Americans, we grew deeper into developing strangers in a violent land.

I am an ordained Elder too. Many churchmen, denominations and laity of the past and today were/are desirous of experimenting with the freedom of religion and other freedoms in an American community. Though congregations on military posts also experienced racially divided services, it was voluntary. When so called Black services, later name changed to Gospel services, began in the 1970's, they overnight became the largest attended worship services on military posts. Began successfully by a black chaplain, their success extended to all military posts and bases. Explained in another part of this book as to why I reluctantly refused such assignment, primarily because it assisted reducing the pressure on white chaplains to find professional and effective adaptations for multiracial congregations. I regretted that African American attendance in military services was percentage wise, very low. Although attendance increased, appointment of non-Chaplaincy endorsed pastors altered the religious and educational requirements for the military Chaplaincy. *Now military Privates or Non-Commission Officers, without college or seminary degrees could create their own congregations, and in many cases transfer their memberships outside the military gates upon retirement or military discharge. There were other complications which I choose to not discuss. Although this added to reports and numbers served and larger Post Protestant Chaplains funds, like in the civilian communities, ministry became "neighborhood" oriented rather than "community" grounded. I determined comparative social issues of civilian communities could transferrable become problematic for military soldiers and their families who must live together and train and fight together as a closely knitted unit.*

For 30 years I escaped the problems of civilian churches attempting to change community folkways and mores. So, it is not a negative complaint against civilian pastors or churches. It is a concern that I raise for questioning whether, as church leaders, we could have been better stewards of our religious respect in America. In free exercise of religion, other faith groups and denominations are without my comment. As United Methodists, the Holy Scriptures, Social Principles, the Discipline and Wesleyan tradition, offered sufficient alternatives to support our US Constitution for racial desegregation of our schools, colleges, housing patterns for community living, local churches, or simply, all that America has to offer for its citizens.

Older Americans saw social tensions of the 21st century coming. They had the wealth but not the energy to prevent it. In the white people I knew during their younger years, they had a positive vision of America, in terms of race. Joel in his book (Joel 2:28, KJV) says: "...*in the last days...your old men will dream dreams, and your young men will see visions.*" Yet farmlands became the newly segregated homes and schools and churches. Lucrative businesses contracted engineers to design new businesses from the growing relocation of assigned white families, under the guise of selling already paid for homes to upscaling nonwhites, to obtain higher mortgages for new purchases. The lure was that your (white) projected property values will increase as other whites desire also to have better schools and safer neighbors.

Some churches were given free land by developers to relocate closer to projected locations for migrating white families. But the wealthy will increase the value of their homes by gating their neighborhoods pending the income level of wealthy families. And, and, and, "Americans of color will be disallowed to racially integrate your community."

Americans of color? Well they can move up to the inflated costs of your run down churches and schools; And after they are in debt with such homes, the banks will participate in redlining their areas; moving out businesses and groceries; depress the value of their lands – until "we" are ready to retake such at the redlined cost - and re-increase the value, of those locations, with higher taxes as the present inhabitants die, with nothing of value, except to leave their children and grandchildren, with used homes in older communities, subpar businesses, run down schools. And don't forget, we also will let the scalpers or the loan sharks; drug peddlers and violent gangs join you to overpower, in those old neighborhoods, a weakened in force police department. Oh, we have plans for them. They will be called "The Wretched of the Earth" by author Frantz Fanon. Nobody will call them blessed anywhere in the world. You and your children will have perpetuated inferiority complexes as all people see and hear on cable television the spoils of victors.

In the First Christian Council, the debate was over "who could come to the Lord's Table." We have not progressed too far from the spirit of that Christian Council in First century A.D.

My disappointment with our institutionalized church rests upon one principle: when a person is misoriented, actions cannot be responsible. The misorientation is at fault but, in the first place, it's the people who allowed themselves to be misguided. I agree that the degree of one's orientation must be consistent with an accepted base. The base of all orientation of the Christian church, under our democratic constitution, is the belief in the Biblical God. Thus, for an American Christian to be correctly oriented, the biblical orientation stems from a Christian principle—The Golden Rule: "Therefore, all things whatsoever ye would that men do to you: do ye even so to them: for this is the law and the prophets..." (Matthew 7:12, KJV)

Following the same rule, if a person ignores our professed God of the Bible, the essence is figuratively turning one's back on God. In addition, if our belief is that to face God is to walk uprightly as a moral being, the vice versa is inevitable. The laws of logic demand coherence. Hence the person who ignores the God of the Bible, even under our constitution, is believed to have an incorrect orientation and follows an immoral path.

The only true task of the church is to present the Gospel and compel people to accept the directives of God. Karl Barth, in his works, postulates that the church exists only because of the spoken Word of God. The foundation of the church is the spoken Word of God. The church has no moral function except the mission of that Word—to evangelize, to make God known.

Whenever any disease is permitted to flourish, a future date for worse complications is in store. For years, the missionary program of the church has expanded. Literally, the church in America, as Jesus commanded, has sent its missionaries to the uttermost parts of the world. Still, even in this effort, justifiable questions have been raised.

In 1971, I attended a United Methodist, military chaplains retreat in Tokyo Japan. Our Divisions of Chaplains coordinated a meeting with a ministerium group of Tokyo. The discussions went great until the question from the American side asked: what can we do for you and your churches? Tempers flared when one Japanese minister said: "Send us physicians; send us scientists; send us teachers, etc., but don't send us anymore preachers or missionaries. It became a heated discussion for in the discussion was accused dishonor for missionaries who died in Japan on the mission field. The Japanese ministers' contention was that the missionaries weakened their nation for the taking advantage of their people by the American government.

I have heard this same argument expressed by natives of Africa and American blacks and made manifest by the history of American slavery. Though the church responded to the call of the military for creating a free Europe, it is accused of being anemic, to the same degree, of defending its evangelized black Africans in the same manner from the evils of aggressive imperialist who happen to have white skin.

Let people criticize my words for what they are. I am under spiritual command to express my thoughts. My thesis is simple. I do not believe the church of Jesus Christ to be irrelevant to contemporary social problems. I understand the frustrations of American students, pastors and laity, past and present, who do not struggle with faith in Jesus but in the Jesus of white America. They mistakenly believe that the origin of our historical knowledge of Jesus which was borrowed from a community who subjected people to slavery and continued social exploitation.

For hundreds of years it has been the Institutionalized Church, that not only expelled Christians from their congregations but closed doors in their faces. It was the teachers of a Christian God that progressively "whitenized" the very nature of God and robbed the distinct personality of a radical Jew, whose skin color is unknown – Thank God! and revolutionized all preconceptions of the Creator of the world. In the eyes of many Christians, the Jesus of history and the Christ of Faith has been constructed into a white man who sanctions the deeds of America, if they do not disturb the traditional patterns of racial segregation, bigotry and discrimination.

I take debate that if God were to speak to finite minds, his medium of revelation of necessity flows through limited channels. By virtue of his unique revelation being experienced in the Jewish community as a race of people is not important. Skin color or contrived race is insignificant. The essential factor is the theological nature of his unveiling himself. I believe that God reveals himself, however limited, through varied means. However, my faith is that "God's highest form of revelation has been seen in Jesus Christ, "... Reconciling the world unto himself,..." (2 Corinthians 5:19, KJV) Archeologists, historians, theologians or other researchers have nothing definitive and can only sell theoretical ideas about the nature of God's divine intervention.

The Gospel has been misinterpreted for personal gain in many historical and contemporary situations, by people of all colors and cultures. An excellent example, "... Love your enemies, bless them that hate you, and pray for them that despitefully use you, and persecute you;" (Matthew 5:43, KJV).

An expressed cause for the exodus from Christian churches is the feeling of the inadequacy of the Gospel to give ample leadership in crucial, obvious, unjust situations. Not so in Korea and Africa where Christian churches are exploding in growth. In America there is discomfort that the basic message of love misdirects persons desirous of justifiable social goals. No. The message that is very clear is that all love must extend beyond neighborhood and into community. It must capture the neighborhood but enwrap the community rather than repel. Do the explosive patterns as the Koreans and Africans justify the advantageous power of racially homogenized communities? My response is perhaps but Americans does not have the option. Ancestors plowed into the lives of another people, forced the intermingling of another people, interchanged the racial DNA with the racial identities, authorized the outpouring of other people from around the globe. Only through another mass genocidal act can reproduce that type of land mass.

The primary fears are that the Gospel enslaves converted members into submission by their oppressors. (Booker T. Washington is quoted as saying that "you can't hold a man down without staying down with him.") One cannot hold another down unless he himself is enslaved." I love one of our Army mottos that said "Lead, Follow, or Get Out of the Way." If American churches do not want to lead," holding up the blood-stained cross of Jesus," it perhaps is time for the church, as an institution, to get out of the way. All people have equal value and integrity, and this should be the most recognizable conviction of the Christian church, regardless of denomination. Yet in America, I agree in free exercise of religion.

I say the Gospel is not enslaving but liberating. I have known few black parents, for example, who unequivocally believed in the supremacy of the white race. Not in the cotton fields; black barber shops; nor on the street corners; never throughout my childhood. Neither did they believe in a black God. They believed in themselves and a colorless and genderless God, though using the accepted language of "He." Many felt socially paralyzed to be liberated from racial confinement, but they believed they were as intrinsically good as anybody else, black or white.

I never shall forget the late Mrs. Mary Jones, mother of my best friend, with lower formal education. People usually in a derogative manner, referred to her as "May Beck." Mrs. Jones was an aged lady. As we were sitting on her porch one afternoon, Mrs. X, an affectionate white lady drove by in a modern, clean beautiful car and exclaimed with a friendly wave, "Hi May Beck!" with all tones of genuine devotion.

Mrs. Jones shouted back, in the same tone, "Hi Mrs. X!" Then in a low begrudging voice, she said, heh, heh, "I'm no May Beck either!"

Another pivotal moment of challenge to impact my life was given by "Mr. Acorn," the perceived town drunk. Seemingly, Mr. Acorn was always drunk and had an open cell at the town jail where he worked off his fines when jailed. A medium brown skin small of stature person, with skimpy stubby beard, his clothing was long sleeve multicolored shirt with tie, regardless of the summer heat, that mismatched everything; baggy dress pants with watch chain that hung from the belt top to his right pocket; wide brim straw hat with sweated brim; Old Crow whisky bottle in his right back pocket; and always playing his guitar hanging from his shoulder, while walking the streets to landscape yards as he pushed his mower with his stomach. He could always find yard jobs.

On this day he allowed me to join him with my mower and would pay me enough for the movies and popcorn and a little extra on large yards ($.25-$.50). On this day in the middle of a black asphalt street in North Winona, in close to 100-degree heat, he turned to me and said: "Davis come up here (we were in single file) you think I'm crazy, don't you? As an eleven or thirteen-year-old, I said: "No Sir! He said: "Yes you do, everybody thinks I'm crazy, but I have more sense than the average person. You know how come I act like this? I act like this because I don't have an education, so I get anything I want from white and black folk by acting crazy." Then with his forefinger forcefully piercing my forehead, he said angrily "Promise me Davis! Promise me you won't stop until you get an education!!!!! Promise me!!!!" "With my head hurting from this instant gesture I said: OK Mr. Acorn!! OK Mr. Acorn!" The imprint of his finger left a feeling even to this day.

The year I was unable to go to college bothered me because of this promise. When things were challenging in seminary, I once considered leaving the seminary. Mr. Acorn's forefinger, keeping my roommate from also quitting, and my promise to Mr. Acorn kept me. Even as an Army Chaplain and while getting a Doctoral degree years later after retirement, this "Acornic" promise kept fueling my energy.

Oh, how I wish he were alive to see the seed he planted. I don't know if he ever attended a worship service at home to hear me preach. All of my churches were outside of Winona and early on I had not felt the full impact of his encouragement and guidance. Before I remembered in later years to remind him of that day and thank him, I learned he was deceased. Strangely I could fine nobody in Winona who knew his real name except "Acorn" the town drunk.

Although some upper-class citizens corrupt the morals of youth, this town drunk had a strong influence in the making of a pastor, a highly decorated Army Chaplain promoted to the rank of Colonel with two Legions of Merritt; a Senior Vice President at one of the largest hospital systems in America and who earned a Doctoral degree.

The traditional black man's orientation of manhood was different from popular western opinion. He had no inferior feelings as to his manhood. Therefore, he felt no urge to exemplify external gestures when one attempted to insult him. Manhood to the traditional knowledgeable black man was to use wisdom above emotions and always utilize only the advantage regardless of the confrontation.

I do not speak of incidents when black men let emotions dominate wisdom and were annihilated. I speak of the majority of blacks who pleaded no revenge or retaliation on their behalf by other blacks in spite of their tragic, unjust plight at the mercy of white. The dominant themes echoed by older blacks of our social environmental plight, regardless of personalities varying from "Uncle Tom's" to passive pessimists; the teaching emphasis was "our day will come."

Muhammed Ali (Cassius Clay) has this relevant analogy: "A man will be a fool, for the sake of bravery, to race full steam ahead to an oncoming fighting bull. People will say "look at that brave man" meeting that bull head on." But the bull will splatter him.

The Gospel has undebatable relevance for our leaders of great political influence, who regard its relevance, to write social laws to guide our multicultural nation. Even they could better understand the crux of our social pathways challenging our citizenry. Were governors more reliant upon the source stated, as that which helped construct our nation, pertinent insights with answers to problems plaguing their states would be more affirmative. And were the people aware of the true meaning of the Gospel, they could better understand the necessities for the 'whys" of political and social change. *"But how can they call on him, if they have not believed? And how can they believe, if they have not heard the message? And how can they hear, if the message is not preached? (Romans 10:4 TEV)*

In a sermon preached to the Upper Mississippi Conference of the Methodist Church, the late Dr. Lowery used Matthew 15:13 *"Every Tree that my Father did not plant will be rooted up.* He entitled his sermon, "Trees are Falling." As an example of plants, he focused on Egyptian slavery of the Jews, American slavery of Africans, Apartheid in South Africa; Jim Crowism and racial segregation in America. He emphasized these as plants not planted by God and would be rooted up.

"THE MYTHOLOGY OF RACISM"

Time Life Books: The Civil War series states the Civil War resulted in 1,100,000 casualties and 620, 000 American deaths. The University of Colorado at Boulder estimates the cost of the Civil War at $6.7 billion; 4 times the total government expenditures from 1789-1860.

There was destruction of the Confederacy, and yet the issue of race is as pronounced today as during the latter years of American slavery. From 1882-1951, although at least 4730 Americans (3437 blacks and 1293 whites) were lynched; especially during the Reconstruction period, the lynching of blacks became acceptable even for church going Americans, led by ordained clergy. The issue of race exacts emotional, spiritual, physical, educational and economic toll today as though the Civil Rights Movement of the 1960's and 1970's never existed. Why? This book explores the psychological dimensions of racism to encourage elimination of the same.

Slave owners, both white and black, in their observation of the physical, intellectual, spiritual and psychological strength of their slaves, knew their slaves were not inferior to white or black people. To reduce contemporary misunderstanding, white, black and brown skins, (before 1660 were called Indentured Servants) even today, are trapped as slaves in the sex trade, politics, forced racial segregation, poverty, criminal markets as opioids or other illegal drugs. And poor whites as well, as poor blacks lack enough health insurance, job security and retirement in prosperous America.

Slavery has never known skin color, today or in yesteryears, except in political fantasies or the creation of racial myths intended on social and class domination. John Hope Franklin in his book "Slavery and Freedom" noted that in some cases before 1860, white slaves in America received harsher treatment from slave owners than their black counterparts. Hired straw bosses whose responsibility was to oversee the work of the slaves, knew beyond reasonable doubt that slaves were not inferior people. Black slaves who could compare themselves with the personhood of white people knew they were not inferior to white people. Racial Segregationists, for the sake of wealth and political dominance, attempt to elevate their social status by spending millions of tax dollars, engaging in moral bankruptcy, to discredit the intelligence and social worth of black people, know and knew that black folk nor white folk are inferior nor superior to each other. Black and white folk, since and before the desegregation of public schools and churches, know and knew that racial inferiority or superiority, purely on racial grounds is a travesty. Historians who attempt to ignore the noble contributions of black folk and at the same time glorify the contributions of white folk, know that black folk are an inalienable part of history and not inferior to white folk. To ignore this fact is to lie on paper, despite knowledgeable truth, to themselves and others, who will listen to them or who are forced to listen to them.

In an Army Chaplain Basic Training class in 1967, I was surprised, perhaps shocked, that we were taught on causes for social insurrections. The objective of the class was providing knowledge to assist, our projected assigned military Commands, in reducing social unrest or rebellion of South Vietnamese during their war against North Vietnam.

I remember standing, in our largest class during the Vietnam war, to make a statement. I admitted being in a state of feeling insulted, that amidst persistent Civil Rights marches, social unrest and citizens pleading and dying for justice in America, we categorically understand the causes, and are teaching them, without correcting our own social order. This is an insult. Our teacher, also an Army Chaplain, agreed with me, and with courtesy emphasized the purpose for the class content was for chaplains to be knowledgeable in performing their ministries. I do not remember peer discussions about the fact except private agreement from my other two African American classmates, who are now deceased. Other classmates came in agreement with me after class.

Wikipedia's short definition of a myth is *"A widely held but false belief or idea." The Random House Dictionary defines it as: a traditionary or legendary story, usually concerned with deities or demigods and the creation of the world and its inhabitants.*

A quotation from my father permeates the ideas of this book that: *"There is no difference between black and white people. Some black men will stab you in the back. And some white men will risk their lives to save you. Never judge a person because of the color of their skin."* Dr. King, much younger than my father, later publicly affirmed what daddy had taught: *"Never judge a person by the color of their skin but by the content of their character."*

There is a allegory, (author unknown), of a man who knowingly captured a baby eagle, placed a weight on its angles, threw it in the chicken yard, to be raised as a chicken. He enjoyed observing its difference from chickens predestined to laying eggs and ultimately the chopping block for food. But the growing eagle noticed a difference also.

Not that he was better than his feathered yard mates, but his features seemed to offer him a different destiny. What to be was upsetting until he saw birds of his own kind soaring the horizon. Yet in recognizing his own strength and capabilities, when he tried to join them, he was weighted down by an imposed, contrived plan. Severely depressed, unannounced a lost hunter was passing and noticed this act against nature, dislodged the weight and departed. Without understanding freedom, but desiring to be like others of his nature, on the next eagle flyover, the enslaved eagle used that which was a natural gift and left the chicken yard forever. He was able to experience what Leontyne Price sang: "I wish that I knew how it feels to be free."

The mythology of racism is that it is not complex but a simple system. An example, Pharaoh of the days of Moses or King Herod in the days of Jesus. Both tried, with failure, to deter future leadership by destroying babies from their abusive use of governmental authority. Their fear was that someone, from a different tribe, would one day dethrone their superior position. Whereas they appeared to be strong, they proved themselves, in history, to be weak losers, by attempting to destroy infants.

The adherents of criminal behavior do not learn from history. Rather they perpetuate the misery of others by "Kicking against the pricks" (Acts 9:5) and, without change, ultimate loss of dignity and a promised trip to the burning fires of Hades. (Matthew 13:42) God is not the author of racism "but of power, love and of a sound mind." (2 Timothy 1:7)

Davis-Tyler Reuniom
2017

REFLECTIONS ON A LIFETIME OF MINISTRY

This book began at my six months of age. Creation did not begin with Sigmund Freud nor would he make that claim. Freud's insight into the human psyche was pivotal in enabling other human beings to have a better understanding of human nature. The contributions of other psychoanalysts, psychologists, sociologists, historians, anthropologists, theologians and the host of specialist in all areas of life provide clearer understanding of our natural order. Yet so much has been overlooked in the lessons taught in Uncle Remus Tales; African Proverbs, etc., and the wisdom that Eric Berne, psychiatrist and author and his school of scholars explain which comes from not trained intellectuals but reflections on *"the woman at the clothes line;"* or in the words of the late Bishop Joseph E. Johnson, New Testament theologian and seminary professor, on *"the wisdom from "Aunt Jane."*

An appreciated definition of education from my, (name forgotten) high school assembly speaker is "The meaning of education is *"to bring out that which is already within."* That which is already instilled within is instilled by God. Consequently, everybody possesses what mankind cannot understand - God's innate gifts, which can only be identified, polished and enjoyed, but never created. Such innate gifts are already embedded in every student before they enter the classroom. The ultimate challenge and responsibility of the teacher is to help identify and cultivate the educational nuggets that are found.

Unfortunately, during the early and subsequent days of school racial integration, reluctance to rise above culture has perhaps destroyed the educational genius and development of an entire generation of America's students. The reluctance of some teachers to maximize their teaching skills with some students, and intuition of that unwillingness by all students, the actions of some students, showing off their refusal to study and learn, has severely hampered secondary education in America. Negative attitudes toward quality education for all who attend classes, has drained educational energy from both student and teacher. In the front page of USA Today, January 14, 2014: "The gifted and talented classes are attended by mostly white and Asian kids; the general education classes, mostly black students." This reference is PS 9 in Brooklyn, NY, not southern USA. I discuss this, what should be classified as a crime against children, in another part of this book.

Although enormous taxes have paid for salaries, buildings, unnecessary busing and educational resources, America loses. Incarceration centers are lacking in supply to maintain space for educational failures which pivot on broken families from broken dreams. The streets or interstate highways, shopping centers nor gated communities, churches nor vacation paradises, are safe from former angry students, intentionally failed by racially bias systems.

At Southeast Institute, Dr. Martin Grober, Psychiatrist, in one of his many lectures, explained it this way. His colloquially use of words explained his "Idiot Scale." He held that the only difference between gangsters, gang leaders, Hitlers, leaders of corporation executives,

Presidents of Nations, college presidents, bishops, military generals, et al, is their orientation. All have very high IQs.

Such IQ executives know the truth about racial equality, yet employ wasted critical resources to enrich their own pockets, self-esteem, and simultaneously degrade our American flag and U.S. Constitution that symbolizes freedom, truth and equal pursuit of happiness. It is this social and corporate behavior, who symbolically spits on our American flag, which is more demeaning than taking the knee, and has given birth to the criminal state of American cities and towns and lack of world peace.

So, where I came from, or to, was arranged by what some call providence. I call it God.

Everybody has a life. Some are short lived; others traverse the years to have over a century of experiences. They are not forgotten. Psycho-neurosurgeons such as Wilder Penfield discovered years ago that nothing a person experiences is ever forgotten. One may lose recall but given the proper stimulus, all past experiences can be recalled just as they happened. I am in hopes that anyone who has experienced me in their past will find meaningful reasons to thank God for positive lessons learned and not be sidetracked by my imperfections, (which are many) that surfaced at a particular time of experience.

Many times, I plotted leaving the ministry because of personal imperfections. But in sermons, readings, or meditation, I listened to *Paul the Apostle: (2 Corinthians 12:8-10, KJV)* "*8 For this thing I besought the Lord thrice, that it might depart from me. 9 And he said unto me, my grace is sufficient for thee: for my strength is made perfect in weakness. Most gladly therefore will I rather glory in my infirmities, that the power of Christ may rest upon me.10 Therefore I take pleasure in infirmities, in reproaches, in necessities, in persecutions, in distresses for Christ's sake: for when I am weak, then am I strong.*"

It is this fact of life that makes you and me who we are today. Some past experiences were painful at the moment, but gracefully redemptive to enable future moments of joy and stability. Inclusive are romantic heterosexual relationships with girls as well as fighting moments that occurred during maturation times with fellows. Consequently, during physical or mental reunions as adults, all is forgiven for by the grace of God we lived to see another day, even unto this day. Eric Erickson's human stages of development, especially the genital phase, also gives me much insight of personal experiences, coupled with the grace of God that has brought me to this point in life.

This book references a lifetime of ministry because like Jeremiah, I also believe I was ordained for ministry before "I left the belly of my mother." I was placed in situations that would direct my steps and protect my life for this moment. I now understand why God must be given the glory for all of life. Of my five closest childhood friends, only two of us are alive today. Of my 28-high school graduation class, only seven of us remain. Of the three African American Chaplains who in June 1967 attended our eleven-week Army Basic Chaplain Training Course of, as I recall, 275 chaplains, I am the only African American with the blessing of life and military retirement as a Colonel.

After only three weeks in Vietnam in 1968, I was assigned to do worship services in Ankhe, VN. Flying treetop level in a Loach helicopter from Camp Enari at Pleiku, through the snaking highway 14 East of Mang Yang Pass, where years earlier the French had been defeated in war, we flew into a Viet Cong ambush of a USA convoy. With "POP! POP! POP!" on the bottom of our helicopter and Chief Warrant Officer Wilcox's instant left/right and vertical turns until reaching an altitude out of danger, he said "Pardon my French Chaplain but I was just shot down yesterday!!!" With hands covering my knees trying to hide my shakes, I admired this young soldier's being back in the air again for our country in support of our troops. I was also aware of how momentarily death could come. My leading of worship for his unit, for me, was even more meaningful.

There are so many instances of my life where death could have exercised a convenience for my termination, Vietnam notwithstanding, yet my life has been spared to write these words and preach the Gospel. Of the many families with 11 children, death has not yet determined a painful reduction in our family for which we are grateful to God and man. That time, like in the lives of other close friends and relatives, will come. So, for now we are grateful for God's grace, not lucky charm or wisdom or even genes. Just gratitude, not for the lucky stars, but God's grace that has been enough for us/me.

Since birth, I had no conscious thoughts or the slightest interest of becoming a pastor or minister. I participated in all jokes heard, and there were many, about "baldheaded preachers. All clergy were highly respected, and *often* invited into our home for social calls and meals by and our parents. My perception of community respect was in this order: the town physicians (all white); the school principal and then the preacher (pastor) all black. But the preachers and their wives always occupied a special value in our black community and were the unquestioned leaders of our churches – white or black. Our United Methodist church did not dissolve its racially constructed Central Jurisdiction until 1968.

At 19 years of age after spending 15 months in Chicago working for cash to return to college in vain, except through the generosity of our older sister, I was now a freshman at Mississippi Valley State College (MVSC) in 1958 with a major in Mathematics. I wanted to become a Civil Engineer and build bridges and accomplish a childhood dream of becoming a millionaire by age 35. (years later in a group, someone reminded me that as a clergy in interracial settings, that's exactly what

I am doing – building bridges and if we live long enough, the benefits of military retirement are worth a million dollars. So, God's grace has the last word.

We cannot survive without people who care about us looking over our shoulders). In the second quarter at MVSC, strange experiences began to disturb me. Every evil, racial or otherwise began to prick my conscious awareness. Even the evils I had witnessed the past year on the streets of Chicago returned to my conscious memory with a vengeance. Moreover, amid the vividness of tragic scenes playing tapes on my consciousness, even in Trigonometry classes, I began questioning my sanity. Strangely, a sermon I had heard months earlier from the text, Joshua 14 with subject "Give Me This Mountain," also became dominant in my subconscious hearing. Reverend Joseph Wells of Chicago had looked as though he was pointing at me in his delivery that Sunday morning at Mt. Pisgah Baptist Church.

(Joshua 14:12-15, KJV)

[12] *Now therefore give me this mountain, whereof the* LORD *spake in that day; for thou heardest in that day how the Anakims were there, and that the cities were great and fenced: if so be the* LORD *will be with me, then I shall be able to drive them out, as the* LORD *said.*

Troubled by these words of Caleb and the persistence of this experience, for some reason I embarrassingly stopped unannounced by retired Methodist pastor Reverend John Wesley's home for assistance with my problem. After listening for a few minutes, Reverend Wesley, a retired District Superintendent of our Methodist Church said, "Davis my boy, don't you know you are being called to preach?" I said "No sir!!! I don't want to be no preacher!!!" He responded "well that's the clearest Call I have ever seen!!! It's up to you what you want to do about it!! God doesn't ask, He directs!!!"

Almost suddenly a scripture I had read in my first and only personal

Bible given to me by Reverend and Mrs. Walter G. Pruitt came to memory from (Ezekiel 3:17-19, KJV): *17 Son of man, I have made thee a watchman unto the house of Israel: therefore, hear the word at my mouth, and give them warning from me. 18 When I say unto the wicked, "Thou shalt surely die; and thou givest him not warning, nor speakest to warn the wicked from his wicked way, to save his life; the same wicked man shall die in his iniquity; but his blood will I require at thine hand. 19 Yet if thou warn the wicked, and he turn not from his wickedness, nor from his wicked way, he shall die in his iniquity; but thou hast delivered thy soul."*

My maternal grandmother was begging us, seemingly since birth, to live right so after her death we would see each other again in heaven. Now I was in the position of defying an order from God and not going to heaven.

I went on for a few weeks with the problem mentally and spiritually escalating until on October 28, 1958 I informed our church pastor ahead of worship services that he "was in my seat." Reverend C.T. Allen instantly became my mentor and pusher. Our church and community respected my decision by instantly giving me the uncomfortable title of "Reverend." I was no longer "Sonny" which sounded with family love, but uncomfortably, Reverend.

In high school I was Elvernice and among close friends, "LD, Davis, Dave or Brother Dave." My father, mother and family, especially my maternal grandmother, who I am told shouted within her home in Memphis, and other members approved, when learning I accepted my Call to Ministry. MaMa's brother had been a Baptist pastor in Water Valley, MS. My brother two years younger than me, now tells his story of being confused, from a dialectical respect, as to how to be a brother of a preacher. We had slept in the same bed since childhood and even dated two sisters. Our dreams were to one day drive across country together, perhaps with those two sisters. Life has its own pathways.

Yet he was no more confused than I as to how to adjust my social life with dating and even talking with friends.

I began to silently question how married clergy had children because of puritanical and religious teachings of the body from home and church. I even personally declared a vow of poverty because the pastors I knew lived below the salary scales of teachers who were the only African American professionals in Winona. I for a period stopped dating because I was no longer in touch with my former prideful self and did not want to enter a romantic relationship with no knowledge of what my future held.

(God has a sense of humor-praise God!) My trial sermon, in November 1958 of which I had no sleep for a week in preparation, was from the book of Jonah, *"When Running from God."* I was appointed as Pastor at the ensuing Annual Conference in June 1959 to the Vaiden Circuit with 3 churches. Without expectation, our Methodist (now United Methodist) connection took over my educational and ecclesiastical progression. (We have a dynamic religious denomination). After Summer Clergy training at Gulfside Methodist Assembly in Waveland, MS, the following year I was transferred to Rust College, our United Methodist College in Holly Springs, MS and appointed to a student pastorate of two churches. Then I was appointed after college graduation to Gammon Theological Seminary in Atlanta, where in my second year I was offered the Crusade Scholarship and student pastorate in South Pittsburg, TN and the remainder is my resume, written by our United Methodist heritage.

So, don't blame me!! Right? Blame God, them, and others for activating their faith in God to produce potentiality what I never knew God had endowed within me. Blame my older sister Rubye for not letting my first year of disappointment, in inability to go to college, not open me for fatal social mistakes. I was singing in a "Duwhop" quartet in Chicago hoping to get a manager to record our two songs and make it big like the Platers, the Moon Glowers, and other big singers. Yet after having social differences, I left the quartet and moved to South Chicago. I am always innocent in blame –right? Aren't you?

I can recall very early in my pastoral ministry one Sunday morning when loading my car for my trip to preach at one of my three churches. Our teenage neighbor, the age of my younger brothers came from his home across the street with tears streaming down his cheeks. He said Sonny, "You are a preacher – right?" I had noticed the sheriff place his father under arrest, again, and drove off with him to the jailhouse. This was a regular Saturday night or Sunday morning ordeal for behavior of his father. Although our Montgomery County was a dry county, alcohol could be purchased openly on my home street and the street behind us. Intoxicated men and women walked the streets, especially after payday on weekends. The bribe, if paid to whoever was elected as sheriff was impossibly not very high. However, the person selected as Sheriff always seemed to pull up economically very quickly. As kids, we always noticed the homes discharging such persons to the streets, stayed in business regardless of elections and intoxicated persons always frequented their same homes.

So, here was our young neighbor crying and saying, Sonny I want to make a promise to you and God: "I will never ever touch a drop of alcohol as long as I live because I see what it does to my father." While still struggling with my Call to preach, I thank God to have represented something of urgency for our neighbor's need. I asked him if we could shake on his promise, he agreed. As youngsters, we also loved and respected his parents.

Fast forwarding to doing my initial months in Vietnam as an Army Chaplain, my mother wrote to me that our same neighbor had been wounded. I located him at the Long Bin Hospital, called and requested the chaplain tell him he was representing me. I had arranged to visit but before I could make it there to visit him, he had died from a fatal improvised explosive device injury. It was almost impossible for me, even today, to withstand the agony of my grief. *Here a young citizen had answered the draft and hoped to financially assist his mom and family. I understand his life insurance, after his death, helped his family to purchase a home.*

This young American, embodied the personality types of so many young Vietnam soldiers of which many, even from Winona (do I need to say black and white?) were killed or wounded in battle during Vietnam. Isn't this black/white thing sickening to you? Then let's drop it in this 21st century!! All of us are Americans!! "Isn't" that enough?? Go to the Vietnam Memorial in Vicksburg, MS or other states, and see the pictures of Americans who died for our flag. I am told the same types of pictures, from that era, reveal an embarrassment in the halls of Congress for the numbers there who found excuses and protection of wealthy or politically connected families to dodge the draft. Now as American heroes they pass laws to protect the flag but in their draft able ages, symbolically spit on the same flag.

In this book I also wish to capture other defining moments that evolved me to become the "Sonny" Davis of today. This book consummates a preference, like the call to ministry, which I feel spiritually overpowered to do. Again, like when I first answered my call to preach, I really didn't want to do it because evil folks don't want their evil deeds exposed. Neither did I. I am not a Saint, had no plans to be one and except by the grace of God was protected from grave errors of my ways as those publicly accused or identified as being evil. I even thought that so called evil people, because of the "good" times I thought they were having, did not want to change. I learned that was, is not true.

I had many plans for my life and many of those plans did not take in consideration the ethics of my extremely conservative home training or God. (My brother Tiny squealed to Muhdear (mother) on me once for saying "Hot dog!" She got my legs with a switch.

We were a conservative family long before conservative became political. African Americans as a race were always conservative to the Bible and Constitution; a fact is that they were largely Republicans because of President Abraham Lincoln. That's all we had, the Bible, the Constitution and the Republican Party prior to political takeover, largely by southerners. Blacks left the party to become Democrats with President John F. Kennedy, and the Dixiecrats, who were white Democrats seized the moment to follow strong Southern politicians for strength in the Republican party. Apolitical, I only felt predestined to become a millionaire by age 35. I was challenged, for survival, to not ignore the teachings of my biological father which mirrored the lessons from Sunday school and sermons forced upon us in church worship.

A pivotal story for me given by my father was one of a buzzard and sea gull. Both were doing well down South and the sea gull convinced the buzzard they could do much better up North. So as soon as they crossed the Mason Dixie line, there was a "Screech! and Bam!!" A truck hit a cow. "Brer Buzzard, your dinner already!" Deciding to wait until the meal was done, the buzzard circled while the sea gull flew to a promising lake for its fill on fish. Suddenly a sanitation truck picked up the cow which left the buzzard in hunger while the sea gull was filled. The same was repetitive. Consequently, as the sea gull was gaining in health and fatness while Brer Buzzard was declining in health and morale, Brer Buzzard declared a position in life. He said, "Brer Sea Gull, what you have promised is true. There is something up north that's dying every day. But I am going back where the living doesn't bury the dead!" Then daddy's teaching point: *There are things that are good for the other fellow or other people, but you have to determine what's best for you!*

Another strong teaching to all of his children inscribed in our memories is "If a bull butts you over the fence the first time, it's the bulls fault; he should have put up a sign or told you he was a fighting bull. But if the same bull butts you over the fence the second time, it's your fault; you should either stay out of the pasture or practice the art of bull fighting because you knew he was a fighting bull."

Providentially, I am who I am because there are so many different teachings from my father (I regret all fathers may not leave their sons with lessons from life) *and* I did not want to disappoint the high moral ideals instilled within by our mother. Yet somehow, I was more concerned about nonalignment with the church and my family tradition than I was with alignment with God. Like teenagers who leave home for the first time, we risk living our own lives free of family restraints.

Change seems painful although the ability to change rest simply upon a decision to do so. To be clear, I have never sought such behaviors such as starting fights. I never wanted and still don't to hurt anybody emotionally or physically and always knew if I got into a fight, as taught by my father, I would think ahead of how to win, even with odds against me. Daddy taught us to try to stay out of fights! *"If you can, run ten miles around a fight!"* But if you are forced into a fight by somebody bigger than you, *"it is better to lay down after one punch rather than be beaten to death. But when you see an advantage, at a later date, "If he is on his knees shooting marbles or turning the corner at night, take a two by four board and knock his brains out of him. He will get the* point."

Sometimes it seems that inflicting pain is often the only way to liberation and freedom. The Old Testament if filled with God's interaction in our world. And yet God somehow spared me the acting out of embedded feelings and thinking so that my perpetrator always stopped before my decision for action was carried out. As an Army Stockade Chaplain and prior visits to jails in my pastoral appointments, I could empathize with inmates who did not have those same teachings embedded in their psychological defense mechanisms.

Today we experience teenagers who commit mass murders with combat weapons following insults and or bullying or brainwashing by political heroes. Such a pity for both the innocent victims and the sickened perpetrator.

It is repetitive for me to say that we have no choice over the circumstances of our birth. The date, place, parents, biological identity and forces that shape our life vocation are beyond our ability to determine. As I have repeated many times, the clarification of God's Call of the prophet Jeremiah is synonymous with my feelings of compulsion in this area of ministry focus. In (Jeremiah 1:5, KJV) God says, *"Before I formed thee in the belly, I knew thee; and before thou camest forth out of the womb, I sanctified thee, and I ordained thee a prophet to the nations."* Not a prophet to the neighborhood. Not to a race of folks. But to a diverse gathering of independent or interdependent communities (nations). Hence, I felt honored to preach and pastor in congregations of Koreans, Montagnard of Vietnam, Germans, Africans, white and black Americans, etc.

It was a blessing for me to be born in a family where I felt nurtured, protected, loved, a deep sense of personal and family pride and independence. In a comical but realistic way, even our first pet dogs, Joe and Polly, both bird dogs, loved and protected us as children. If our parents chose to discipline us as children, they had to close the doors to our home because when hearing us crying, Joe literally would attempt to scratch the front door down with barks and moans while attempting to come to our rescue. These truisms became strong walls that sheltered me from the harshness of the world outside of family. Yet, these walls had doors through which I had the freedom to experience the world outside but would always feel welcome upon return and receive psychological bandages for any wounds inflicted while outside those walls.

I was able to know the love of my maternal great grandfather and paternal great grandmother. Both were economically independent in that they owned their own homes and enough land for their children to inherit. Both maternal and paternal sides of my grandparents offered a sense of pride and strength enough to protect us from the viciousness of a harsh and racially biased society. My paternal grandparents were separated before my birth and neither ever remarried.

I remember my paternal grandfather for his wearing of expensive clothing in defiance to societal norms for African American men in a highly controlled racial society in Vaiden, Mississippi. Throughout the family grief, from tragic deaths of two paternal uncles and a paternal aunt, the Davis family was known for its strength, pride, independence, and refusal to submit to aggression from either white or black people.

Once in my late teens while visiting Vaiden, the town of my birth, several white men, from my resemblance of Daddy asked: "Boy are you a Davis? Are you B.F.'s boy?" Yes Sir! "Boy you should be proud to have the best black daddy, black or white! You look just like him. You tell him this white man said so!!" Having heard the history of how and why we left Vaiden for Memphis but moved back to Winona, 11 miles north of Vaiden, internally I beamed with pride. Today I still thank God for his grace and the quality of white citizens who believed in fair play and our U.S. Constitution, enabling daddy to live until 78 years old without prison or a lynching.

The strength of the maternal side of my family lay in their ability to be a strong, respectable, independent, hardworking, land-owning family. My maternal great- grandfather owned a large, successful farm. My maternal grandfather owned a home with acreages within the city limits of Winona, Mississippi. Today a small street in my hometown is named in his honor. My maternal grandmother was a schoolteacher and voracious Sunday school teacher and Bible student. As long as I can remember "MaMa, she wanted all her "Piggies" to be baptized (under the water) so she could see us again in Heaven.

What this means to me is that in an era when the image of strong African American males was an inherent challenge to a white male dominated society, male and female models in our family offered strength, determination, strategy for survival and feelings of independence to cope with the racial and other social challenges of our social environment.

I know now it was no accident, that since childhood, I experienced racial integration and acceptance in a racially segregated social environment. Not only was there racial segregation, but the state of Mississippi was nationally and internationally renowned as being the worst racial state, (other people's description), or environment in America. Yet in Mississippi, there were the best and worst of times. The illustrations given below are to contend that whites and blacks are closer as friends and neighbors than public media portrays them to be. I believe, on a deeper level, racial intolerance is not and never has been the force causing the outplay of public endorsement. There is rather a constraint within our society that blinds the eyes of the mind, places a type of psoriasis on the emotions to enable the committing of heinous acts that afterward one is too embarrassed and fearful to admit. So, history books and public testimonials are discouraged though similar acts are repetitious, even in the 21st century. Consequently, people who were made to be human become instead like robots, unless outside of the public eyes.

INTERRACIAL ACTIONS BEST OF TIMES

It was the best of times, when Leontyne Price, of Mississippi, could recall a white family providing financial resources for her education which led to her becoming a world-renowned opera singer. It was the best of times, at least for me, in 1962 when the governor of Mississippi declared "Willie Richardson Day" in Jackson, Mississippi. The honor was rare for an African American person, although this African American wide receiver of Jackson State College, led the South in receptions to win the football game between the North and the South, and was also awarded MVP.

It was the best of times, when Hodding Carter led the fight for civil rights for all citizens from his newspaper, the Greenville Delta Democrat, and won the Pulitzer Prize in 1946. Mr. Carter, of Greenville, Mississippi remained defiant of the Mississippi racial culture.

It was a personal best of times, when on October 1, 1961, while students at Rust College, Holly Springs, Mississippi, in travels to an interracial Methodist Student Movement Conference in Atlanta, GA, Nathaniel Green and I were encouraged by the white cafeteria patrons to eat breakfast in the white cafeteria of the Greyhound Bus Station of Birmingham, Alabama. Their actions encouraged us to defy the white policeman, who was resisting compliance with the National Commerce Commission (NCC) ruling. The NCC's ruling to racially desegregate was operative starting at 12:01am after midnight on that day. Suddenly after 5:30am, the cafeteria was filled with white policemen who after Nat and I left the table of two uniformed army white soldiers who invited us to be their guests, were violently thrown out of the cafeteria. We made national radio news that day as two African American college students who desegregated the Greyhound bus station of Birmingham, Alabama.

It was a best of times in 1963 when twenty-three white pastors in Jackson, Mississippi, including Dr. Maxie Dunam, presently on staff of Christ United Methodist Church, Memphis, TN wrote a letter to the Jackson Daily News, denouncing the racial conditions in Mississippi as intolerable. Many were ordered to leave the state by the White Citizens Council. What they did was for others, but as I often tell Maxie, he did it for me. Pastors who are white were emotionally elevated in my respect for their Call to preach the Gospel. Before then, because of social conditions, to me, white pastors were *rather imposters* of the Gospel.

It was the best of all times, when a white man saved our home from foreclosure after under the tutelage of Medgar Evers my brother and I joined the Student Chapter of the NAACP at Rust College in 1962. This white man and my father, in Mississippi, had been friends and played ball together as young men. As I explain later in this book, it was playing football, in our yard, and wrestling with Mote Knight, a white kid my age about 11 or 12, who shattered my belief in African American Superiority. Racial integration dispels the notion of White or Black Supremacy, and racial powerbrokers know it.

It was the best of all times, when Mr. and Mrs. Carl Brown (World War II Veterans), and Mrs. Ann Sykes, and Mrs. Taylor of Brown Department Store in Winona, Mississippi, attempted many times, to shield my emotions from the intended hurt of racial slurs, by customers, beginning in my pre-teenage years while working in the same store from 1951-1962. Mr. Brown hired me at 11 or 12 years old as janitor and at 15 let me manage the shoe department and stock boy for the whole store. He carried me on fishing trips *and* business trips to Yazoo City, MS.

I remember when as a growing teenager, I asked if I could talk with him about a personal problem, several times he closed the store earlier so we could talk. I don't remember the conversations except sometimes there were tears. I am the oldest boy of 11 siblings and my father was then working in Chicago. I now know they were typical teenage maturation issues. However, we would talk for over an hour until he asked: "You ready to go home now? And would drive me home for the night. In retrospect, Mr. Brown over the years had become a surrogate father and, in some fashion, I became a surrogate son among their four younger daughters. A tremendous honor and grievous moment were the invitations to me by their family to co-*officiate both of their parents' funerals in* Winona.

It was the best of times, when Mr. Ed O'Neal, a white vegetable farmer, in his affirmation and encouragement for me, as a teenager, to get an education, modeled as we picked vegetables on his farm that "redneck" is a condition of "working in the sun" and not a racist philosophy of life. I saw his neck turn pink where his straw hat did no cover as we picked vegetables in the heat of the day from his field. *Mr. O'Neal once received permission from our mother for me to stay in his home to work and eat at his family table, and sleep in a bedroom in their home, while Mrs. O'Neal attended Summer classes.* This was not classic Mississippi, in that day.

It was the best of times when ants got into my lunch as a daytime cotton picker in his field, and Mr. Jimmie Kent invited me to eat lunch at his family table and requested his same age daughter, probably 13, to entertain me with riding his horse while he napped before returning me to the field. (For 21st century readers, this was usually unparalleled in Mississippi during those years.)

It was the best of times, when Dr. Clarice T. Campbell, our white history professor at Rust College, risked secretly bringing white students, under the cover of darkness, to Rust College from the history class of the University of Mississippi in 1962 to discuss, with a select group of African American students in her History class, ways of improving the social quality of life in Mississippi. It may have been students from Dr. James Silver's History class. He would later write his book: "Mississippi a Closed society."

In July 1965, I was driving from seminary in Atlanta to my pastorate in Aberdeen, MS with TN license plates on my car. Out of nowhere a white man in his 50's or 60's was trailing me for 15 miles with his flashing headlights, two long guns in his back window, Confederate flag on front plate of his truck; and arm waving for me to pull over to the side of the highway. I knew better. He only backed off my rear bumper when I faked motioned pulling a gun out of my glove compartment. But he trailed me all the way until I pulled into the driveway at my parsonage in Aberdeen. I knew my option of going first to the police station would have been tragic for me. Getting out of my car, I first spoke to my African American neighbor across the street and then to him who was red faced and snarled, "Didn't you see me trying to pull you over for 15 miles?" I said: "I looked for a highway patrol symbol and didn't see one and knew you were not talking to me." He said: "you were speeding." I said: "thank you sir for being concerned for my safety, I'll have to watch that." *Getting even redder faced, he said "you are a smart "racial slur" eh? Well you won't get away with this one!!! We'll get you!!"* And with leaving black tire marks on the pavement, he pulled off.

I had politely thanked him for the warning, re-entered my car, drove to Mr. Jackson's home, a parishioner, and borrowed his high powered rifle, swore him to secrecy, returned to the parsonage, went to bed early, set the clock alarm for 1am, with an intense prayer for the potential perpetrators, raised the front window and behind the curtain, awaken with the alarm and with rifle at the ready, waited for hours, and then the next few nights, all prepared for action. All the memories of my paternal grandmother's head injury from being hit in the head with a gun; Emmitt Till's death; Charles Mack Parker's taken from jail and lynched, etc. took over my spiritual consciousness and I was ready for revenge. At that moment I forgot about meeting my grandmother in heaven. Revenge was worth an *eternity in not pursuing heaven.*

I think it was the next week I decided to break up the ground and plant the parsonage's garden spot alongside the road beside the parsonage. Who did I see pass that morning, but the same guy in his, as I remember, pickup truck with racked shotguns in the back window? I waved, he refused and stayed red faced. Every subsequent weekday morning and afternoon at the same time he passed on his way to and from work, for 25 months, still no waving back. Surprisingly, he lived down the street from the parsonage. For two years when seeing him, I always waved to no change of gesture on his part. However, God had delivered me from letting my anger get the best of me.

It was a best of time because I will never forget that the people, as in my childhood, we plan to fight against and kill, if necessary, are usually our own neighbors, right down the street, who Jesus says we must love, and forgive.

It was another intriguing best of times for me to realize in retrospect, his description fit the description of a white person who was inherently angry about his social status in America. Even though he did not realize I had grown up with Americans of his own race and social status, and was taught to understand, respect and love them, we were at a dangerous crisis point. I had pictured the first gun sighting of my retaliation would be the reddened face of my "neighbor" down the street from the church parsonage, where I preached the love of God. Since birth, I had been taught "Thou shall love they neighbor as thyself." What a contradiction. What a tragedy it would have been for my neighbor and me. At that moment, I was not thinking or feeling inclined to model Jesus on the cross saying: "Father forgive them for they know not what they do!" (Which is an indication of an "osis" rather than an "ism." A sickness rather than a belief, which I will discuss later in this book.

Why was this a best of times? It was also because of a similar experience returning to Atlanta following this same coincidence with my white neighbor, as I had come from Atlanta. The church had paid me less than 25 dollars of a fifty-dollar salary that Sunday, mostly in change and small bills. Including my briefcase, all my luggage in the car was empty for refilling after a week for the last trip back from Atlanta to Aberdeen. It was another best of times when on this last trip from Aberdeen, MS to complete requirements for my Bachelor of Divinity degree in Atlanta that year 1965. Racial tension in Aberdeen and the South could be cut with a knife. Siren and lights blasting the quiet darkness, I was stopped in the middle of nowhere, in the late dark of night of Alabama, for my first time as a driver, by two white highway patrolmen. The speed limit after dark on two lane highways across Alabama was 50 miles per hour. On this day before leaving Aberdeen, a parishioner persuaded me to place his 32-caliber pistol on my car seat for protection. Throughout the South as stated in the white neighbor above, white men had double- and single-gun racks for shouldered weapons, and Confederate flags clearly visible in their pickup truck windows or front license plates.

Very nervous to have a visible weapon on the car seat, after dark I had placed the gun on the passenger seat, decidedly, into my briefcase which meant that the briefcase was now empty, except for a loaded 32 caliber pistol, even without my bible anywhere in my car. About 10:30pm in the middle of nowhere, with TN license plates on my car, in the middle of Alabama, suddenly there were the flashing police lights – too close for me to pull the gun out of the briefcase. In panic, as soon as I pulled over, I was out of my car and at the bumper of the two white patrolmen. "Hello preacher!! You are a preacher, aren't you? "Yes Sir, I answered." To all the subsequent questions I responded, sweating profusely, knowing a loaded gun was in my briefcase and not even a Bible among the empty luggage, and only spending change in my possession, a black man with two white police officers, in the middle of nowhere.

Then sitting on his front fender, he asked my opinion on the racial strife. I explained my interracial background and teachings and theological convictions. He then responded how he was raised by his black Nanny and how he loved her, perhaps more than his mother, who spent less time with, him and he had "No problems with African Americans because she taught him to respect everybody." The conversation went on for "years" seemingly, thinking ultimately, he would ask to search my car. After a "lifetime" of sweaty conversation, he asked his partner for his thoughts who returned, "It's up to you!" He said: "preacher we are not going to give you a ticket, but you stayed on the outside of that yellow line too long going into that curve! Now you drive on to Atlanta and drive safely." And as he was walking to his car door, he said, "And Reverend I think you were speeding!" I knew I was guilty of driving above 60 mph and asked to not let me hide behind being a preacher, which I meant. Yet with less than twenty dollars in the car, I would have been taken to jail or worse had the gun been discovered. A search of the car would have been tragic and devastating.

Shaken from the ordeal, I drove not faster than 45mph until I reached Interstate 20.

God's grace gave me another chance and for me to see the inside of another human being, representing everything I had been taught at home, who happened to be white and in a position of legal authority. Upon returning to Aberdeen, I placed the Bible in my briefcase and committed to always have a Bible in the car even until this day.

That night was the best of times. I thank God for the legal angel who pulled me over that night, who happened to be white. It was perhaps that very night that made it easier years later for me to honor the Geneva Convention's mandate and teachings at our Army Chaplains School that noncombatants do not carry weapons in battle.

Contrary to that commitment, under unique circumstances in Vietnam, I refused encouragement to place a handgun in my Chaplains Kit in case our helicopter crashed in the jungle. Except after ministering to a soldier who had been mauled by a tiger, for a short period of time in Vietnam I placed a 45 in my Chaplains kit (under the Bible) to hide it from soldiers. After a few weeks I returned it to the arms room. When visiting soldiers in the field, when asked how I could travel without a weapon, I always replied, "Because you guys are out here and doing a great job protecting us." While carrying a weapon against the Geneva Convention's mandate and the mandate of our church's Division of Chaplains, my personal guilt was a depressing feeling. Moreover, Reverend Pruitt who had given me my Bible had said to me: "Even being on the road at night and day, I decided to not carry a weapon. I trust God because while you are driving, the enemy shoots through the car window or places a bomb under your car or home. A gun unless you are stranded on the road, is not helpful under many circumstances."

It became further the best of all times there in Aberdeen in 1965, when the white Presbyterian pastor, Reverend Tom Carter, encouraged my racial desegregation into the Aberdeen Mississippi Ministerial Association, to bring relief to social changes with minimum racial anguish thereafter. Tom recognized me and pursued with my reluctant call, because of racial tension, during a hospital visit. We had met as fellow inter-seminary movement students in Atlanta, he at Columbia Theological Seminary and me at Gammon Theological Seminary. It was successful because Reverend Reynolds Cheney (Episcopalian), Reverend Charlie Wiggins (United Methodist), The First Baptist pastor (whose name I have forgotten) and other white pastors encouraged and supported the move. Only one other black pastor agreed to join. As an integrated Ministerial Association, we accomplished desegregation of the police force, radio broadcasts, pastor's breakfasts, and the reduction of a radical hostile racial climate. Such positive actions were enhanced with cooperation and a timely production of news articles and a letter to the community by our Ministerial Association, by the editor of the local newspaper, Jim Lacey. These types of positive white clergy and laity led actions, who had an ear to the power structure, are often overlooked by the media and history of black led social involvement.

It was the best of all times, when in 1973, the Methodist Conferences of Mississippi, of which I am an ordained Elder, decided to racially desegregate the structure of our Methodist churches in Mississippi through Conference merger. These best of times which impact my Call to this ministry focus, are by no means exhaustive.

Contrary to the best of times, the other side of the coin also existed in the state of Mississippi. As stated earlier in this book, as a teenager, I remember groaning in spirit over the lynching of Mack Charles Parker for allegedly raping a white woman in 1959. I can still remember in the newspaper the smiling faces of those suspicious in the death of Emmet Till in 1955. I remember the smiles in the media of Byron De

La Beckwith, convicted murderer of Medgar Evers, and the white men joking with him in discussion during the mock trial for Medgar's killing. It seems like yesterday, when Mississippi media exemplified, especially to the African American community, no shame, in the deaths of Michael Schwerner, James Chaney and Andrew Goodwin, the three Civil Rights workers brutally murdered in Philadelphia, Mississippi in 1964. The movie: *"Mississippi Burning" was an emotional theatrical portrayal of that tragic event.*

I remember the desegregation of the University of Mississippi which caused President Kennedy to nationalize the National Guard to protect James Meredith's right for admission in 1963. In 1957, President Eisenhower's nationalization of the same at Little Rock, Arkansas protected the black students who racially desegregated Central High School. President Eisenhower's actions enabled me at 17 years of age to change a lifelong, unannounced, personal, social conviction, and re-decided on a bar stool in a drug store, downtown Chicago, to answer the draft to military service if ever called. Prior to his action at Little Rock, I was still prepared to die for refusal to be drafted to defend racially hostile America from enemy attack.

I remember always having schoolbooks marked by white students the year before because black students could not receive new books at our school. For repetitive emphasis, I remember never believing I would reach adulthood because, as stated, I was prepared to not stop until I killed any white man who would kick me, as other black men were sometimes kicked in public. I now understand the psychological impairment of black rage which began in me as decisions made as far back as 6 months of age. (See Teaching TA Member Mary Goulding's Redecision Therapy later in this book).

WHY STRUGGLE WITH MEMOIRS

For some reason, I never wanted to be important. I was pleased to just be me, outside of the public's eye. Yes, I am reluctant to even write this book because some of you think you will be angry at me. Yet I know the anger is misdirected because, I hope, truth is embodied within the message I am attempting to deliver. And rather than be ensnarled with the enslavement of anger, Jesus in John 8:32, *KJV* says "Then you will know the truth, and the truth will set you free."

Free people are not angry at the object that sets them free. In an afterthought, they always, even like the Centurion at the cross of Jesus in Matthew 27:54, KJV say in reflection: "Surely he was the Son of God!" Heroes are generally recognized after the assassination, not while they are doing their great deeds So, the true anger of protestors of anti-human causes is usually unknowingly directed at themselves for allowing themselves, with all their intelligence, to be misled, even to the path of Hades. One of many definitions (Remember I did not originate the definition; attributed as an Arabian Proverb and many other well-known persons) that "A fool is one who knows not and knows not that he knows not and should be shunned." I've heard it quoted from many pulpits. Occasionally all of us at one time were crazy and we paid the terrible price. On the day of his assassination, I remember media reports that in some southern schools, cheering and clapping at the news that President John F. Kennedy was assassinated *were* recorded. History teaches very plainly that dealing with misoriented people is a dangerous game. There is nothing worth cheering about a President of our United States being assassinated. Perhaps Jesus' words said from the cross, is appropriate here: "Father forgive them for they know not what they do!" (Luke 23:34, KJV)

My father, while shaving, always joked about himself being "such a good-looking man." He compared himself to King Solomon who in Songs of Solomon *1:5-6, KJV* describes himself: *"I am black but comely O daughters of Jerusalem, … Look not upon me because I am black…"* And neighbors, especially ladies, constantly said to me" You look just like your daddy B.F.!" So, if daddy thought he was good looking, which I did too (despite his being darker than me, and that's difficult), by default I reasoned I must also be good looking. (Traits passed down from parents are critically important to a child). I also noticed as I matured, I never had difficulty with admiration from or having dates with the most beautiful of girls, light or dark skinned.

Transactional Analysis teaches that children are dependent upon an overly supply of positive strokes (recognition) every day to survive. So even being of dark skin in a light skin or white society, or being skinny in a muscular, athletic world, could not forge negative penetration within me. Along with Muhammad Ali, before he popularized the phrase "I am the greatest!" I always said that to myself. When I worked in cotton fields, leaf raking, mowing yards, picking up pecans, picking vegetables, or in an air-conditioned store from eleven to 21 years of age, adult positive compliments were soaked in like a sponge for permanent influence. The harsh words received from some customers, though remembered and forgotten, became laughable to me as though the sender was the one who was inconsequential.

The world of children today is extremely harsh, and perhaps has always been for those without strong, positive parental or older sibling protection. And with the tragically high incarceration of physically and psychologically strong African American males, African American youth are in greater danger with feelings of personal lostness. And this pressurized negative reinforcement from the society is emotionally destructive. For example, many crimes, school dropouts, pants below the hip line, I believe, are simply temper tantrums of frustrated children from an oppressive environment. We have sick people because we have a sick society.

My best childhood friend, without a biological father figure in his home, though a tremendous athlete, felt inferior due to his height. He was last in academics of our class. I did not understand his self-inflicted inferiority as youngsters. I found myself encouraging him at every turn. He considered me a true friend, and I was, even until his death. I had the tough honor of eulogizing Ray who never overcame his feelings of inferiority. Ray became a licensed TV repairman and auto mechanic. Yet he never appreciated himself. I always emphasized why he should have become the preacher because he forced me each Sunday to attend Baptist Training Union class where he served as President in our senior year of high school. I now understand the eternal power of negative social scripting and wish for him the reversal had been true.

A tragic example is the daily bombardment of USA racially motivated driver phrases aimed at school age children, especially black children, which is a spiritual tragedy that I wish courts would legally declare socially criminal. (Socrates was forced to drink hemlock for "corrupting the minds of the youth.") Today there is seemingly only commendations for corrupting the minds of black youth by media and to a greater degree police violence.

For example, Mary and Robert Goulding's teachings, (Teaching

Members of TA), as guest lecturer at Southeast Institute, Chapel Hill, NC, offered nine of what she called "Driver Behaviors that must be eliminated for Re-decision Therapy to be effective. Re-decision Therapy is psychotherapy which enables the patient to regress to an earlier state of life; where negative decisions were made to destroy feelings of being OK about self; or declare others as not OK; and to re-decide to be different in the present than the contemporary negative images of earlier decisions. Bob and Mary were leaders in a weekend training workshop in (TA) while I was a student at Southeast Institute. The group consisted of Psychiatrists, Psychologists, Registered Nurses, Social Workers, Clergy and others, all dedicated in helping agencies. Volunteers were asked to do personal work on any issue that had bothered them for a long time. I decided to take the risk.

I permitted myself to be regressed to a deeply emotional time, when as a 6-month-old baby. I had difficulty as to why, for a long time, I felt and looked for excuses to bring about tragic outcomes.

I was regressed back as a 6-month-old to that awful crisis time, which I described and would examine my immature decision. As mentioned earlier, I seemed to wish for a white man to kick me so I could retaliate with murder.

My regression carried me back to that time as a baby when crying, unnoticed, from the room where my two older sisters, mother and *paternal great* grandmother were told to hide. I crawled to my *paternal* grandmother crying as she dealt with white angry men. As she picked me up, she was hit in the head with a gun and I was told she was never the same again. As stated earlier in this book, she nor I were ever the same again. *(This experience was confirmed by my mother with a slightly different remembrance of my sister who was then four years old; but both confirmed the exchanges of me crying, being picked up and the gun hitting incident).* "I was asked *"What did you decide?"* I said I will find the man who hit her and kill him. *"How will you know?"* He will be the one who kicks me. *(This was a growing unconscious strategy to obey that childhood decision)* that ripened with age – babies couldn't figure that out)) I will load my father's gun, find the man to kill and with ammunition complete the act, and hide in my grandfather's woods, and kill the perpetrators until they killed me. *"Are you aware that he is now dead and perhaps in eternal punishment?"* I had never thought about that! Anger in a child just want revenge. So, in the here and now, I took, as invited, soft bats, set up a chair where I imagined his face, (no facial features developed, only a white body) and beat the faceless perpetrator, with emotional name calling, until I was literally sweating and exhausted. I was then invited back to the group, asked my resolve and resolved to get on with my life. I acted out my (crazy) anger in the safety of colleagues in my group. (In my mind, if not killed him; with such a beating I got revenge). The Group therapist then enabled me to redecide a heathier outcome as a mature, informed adult in the here and now. I have now forgiven him, yet, have not been able to forget. What an emotional time I had dealing with the full range of emotions without endangering myself or my perpetrator, (who I now know is answering to God for his misdeeds)

Oh, if everybody had the opportunity to resolve tremendous pressures from unresolved personal issues. *"I praise thee; for I am fearfully and wonderfully made; Marvelous are thy works; and for that my soul knoweth right well.* (Psalm 139:14, KJV) Some psychiatrists, agreeing with Penfield, express belief even in pre-natal decisions of unborn babies. The Apostle Paul has meaning in "When I was a child..." (1 Corinthians 13:11, KJV)

The driver behaviors, called injunctions (always from a strong Parent to a developing Child, in the language of ego states - and they are unconscious messages being sent and received). Such injunctions are: *"Don't be; Don't be you; Don't; Don't be smart; Don't be important; Don't succeed; Don't think; Don't feel and Don't succeed.* These behaviors proceed from strong biological or environmental parental type influences with such psychological pressure that the child at an early age feels threatened if violation of the teachings occurs.

Any child that does not have enough positive input to counter these societal (and often biological) parental negatives that media forces upon them, has extreme difficulty throwing them off to receive the God given prize of human decency. Parents who pass such messages are mostly unaware, and their parents were also unaware of sending them. However, once such messages are revealed through maturation or training, the social environmental Parent, I believe is guilty of corrupting the minds of the youth. Perhaps, even without knowing, I believe this is our father's reasoning, not a formal educator, took time to teach us from childhood to "respect people not by race, but the content of their character."

I believe this is the primary problem influencing school dropout, pre-mature pregnancy, gang banging, adolescent criminal behaviors, youth suicide, homicide and incarceration which all relate to the social disease stemming from complications of devastating societal and or biological parental injunctions.

If Socrates was forced to drink poison hemlock for corrupting the minds of the youth, perhaps if the lawyers of our nation loved children enough, (more than the contractual charges for legal representation) they or political representatives would construct laws sufficient enough to protect our children by "dredging the swamp"), of this modern curse of media injunctions from the bedrock of American society.

There is no haven for Black children in America to shield them from the racial injunctions as described by the Gouldings. And in a society where all great people of history, including Jesus and the biblical patriots, since the late 18th century, have been purposefully painted as white or European, on religious and social media, too many black children and generation Y and Z parents have lost interest in the Christian church and Christian theology due to perceived and well-founded hypocrisy. It is totally impossible for intelligent people worldwide to not see through the less than scientific research that went into evolving white supremacy as a world order. Intelligence is a natural gift where inductive and deductive logic are divine gifts. All it takes is living. So, with TV and public schools, all the racially segregated churches or communities, such staunch refusal to acknowledge in written and televised media the same, it is extremely difficult to reverse the intentional negative and inbreeds into the naivetés of children. As Berne writes in his book on Intuition, children know when something is not right or safe, but have not developed intellect enough to comprehend and express it.

To ancient disciples, Jesus said: "And you shall know the truth and the truth shall set you free." (John 8:32, KJV) Such knowledge means that even if preachers/pastors, teachers, politicians refuse to speak the truth, (to power or their congregations or constituency) church members or constituents are the primary spiritual protectors of their souls and moral strength of their nation. Church members can distinguish between right and wrong without consultation from religious or political leaders. They don't need me to preach the truth of the Gospel and Ezekiel 3 is clear, that God still holds me, as the Called preacher, responsible as ordained clergy.

Believing that the rapture is near, just dangerously could be justification for not being willing to fight against evil destroying every community in our nation and world, rich, poor, black, white, etc. Preaching "The Rapture is near is synonymous to a cartoon I saw of a bearded street wanderer with a sign: *"The rapture is near, bring me your tithes!*" Evidently, there is much work to be done before God rescues us with his Rapture.

Why then am I writing memoirs from the past of a person, me, who feels that without personal perfection, I have done nothing but live the life of complimentary pushes by hand, voice and dollars by others?

Had it not been for the demands of my oldest sister, I had let myself give up on going to college. Were it not for Muhdear's (mother) reminder that "the darkest hour of the night is just before dawn;" and Daddy's *"if you wake up and your hand is in the loin's mouth, you have to take it easy, while getting it out – if you are concerned about your hand."* Had it not been for my promise made to Winona's town drunk, Mr. Acorn, after his threatening insistence that I "Not stop until you get an education!" I perhaps would not have continued when the going got tough in college and seminary, small church parishes, Vietnam away from my wife and 6 months old son or even studies at the doctoral level.

In addition to Mr. Acorn, at seventeen years of age, I tried to slip into a 16th Street Bar in Chicago, and without knowing me, the bartender said "Sonny go home to your mother and drink a glass of milk! A female streetwalker said, "Son I can see you are from a nice family, don't ever come back to a place like this! Find you a beautiful, nice and clean girlfriend!" Trying to talk jive to camouflage my true age, I asked how long have you been in places like this? She replied: "One night is too long, so you get out and I don't want to ever see you in places like this again!! I asked her name and she said "Dorothy." Her mothering talk impressed me so powerfully, I tried to find her again to talk, because what she said hit me emotionally hard. I learned that was only her street name. Yet here was a street walker trying to protect the son of parents she didn't even know.

I had thought bars and "ladies of the night" were where the great action was and filled with evil people. Strangely enough five years later after my first year of seminary, in New Orleans, Dr. Walter Carder assigned me to interview bar dwellers a radius of five blocks from his church – First Street Methodist Church. Thinking I would be unaccepted upon identity, I was welcomed by both men and women with their stories which were life changing. These were the "Low Lives" as called by some upper-class church folk. They were the "But for the grace of God, so would I" people I learned to respect with prayer and wise counsel when opportunity presented itself. Please re-read another life changing perception of people in this book when I was challenged to interview the "Businesswomen" of Korea as an Army Chaplain. All people are beautiful. Ray Stevens popularized the realistic song: "Everything is beautiful in its own way." Many are victims of circumstances up and down the class or racial scales. For this reason, Christ died on the cross. I once read a quote: "There is so much good in most of us; and so much bad in all of us; that there leaves no room to talk about any of us."

Had it not been for strong encouragement by, Chaplain (COL) Conrad walker, my Army Division Chaplain when I became angered by an unwanted, and without discussion with me, a Post Chaplain assignment to start a Black Gospel Service and decided to leave the Chaplaincy, I would not be a retired Chaplain with the rank of Colonel. My stated position was for white chaplains to acculturate themselves to black congregations as I was forced to do for effectiveness to whites of the same. The other requested option was to assign me to pastor only black soldiers and their families or go back to pre-1948 military days although it was now 1974.

Again, had it not been for a white devoted Christian Registered Nurse, Ruth Boshee, attending my worship services at Fort Hood, TX and each Sunday literally unknowingly "hugging the racial stench out of her pastor," with the words, "Thanks pastor I needed that sermon today!" I would not be who I am today. Had it not been for my marital family of 32 years standing by me, and my present wife of 17 years who also as a trusted friend, pulled me out of personal emotional failure and giving encouragement for a happy and successful future, I know I would not be where I am today. Had it not been for ... Had it not been for ... "Had it not been for the Lord who was on our (my) side ...., (Psalm 124:2, KJV)" I would not be where I am today.

Consequently, I write to encourage others to trust God to get beyond the racial injunctions of the evil powers of the devil. Yes, the devil who is un-believed in by many but who at the same time let themselves worship and operate under prescribed devilish influences.

Jesus taught in Luke 6:44, KJV: "each tree is recognized by its own fruit." In the wilderness temptations of Jesus, (Matthew 4:1-11, *KJV*) the perpetrator is called the devil. The temptations were to deny God for promises of *power, wealth and influence.* These three temptations incorporate all devilish influences that come before individuals of the 21st century. They are in sharp contrast to the fruits of the Spirit as pinned by the Apostle Paul in Galatians 5:22-23, *KJV*: "But the fruit of the Spirit is love, joy, peace, forbearance, kindness, goodness, faithfulness, gentleness and self-control." In the image of God, these are our natural human traits until devilish or un-natural influences are permitted.

In TA language, Eric Berne agrees that human beings, in infancy, are "Born OK but their parents (parental type influence) turn them into frogs." The baby is born positively congruent with nature – outside of societal norms, - but under parental pressures, becomes incongruent with nature under the restraints of societal norms. (Folks, so-called racism in un-natural. It has never been congruent with nature and we know it. That is the reason it takes all the crime, billions of dollars, and violent anger to attempt keeping it in place!!!) Once we are affected, not OK and we then spend the rest of our lives trying to become OK again, but while living in agreement with the myth embedded within so called "racism," which is *impossible*.

The reality is not *Racism*, and for my thesis of 1977 at Southeast Institute, was overjoyed in 2019 to see Robin Diangelo write a book on *White Fragility "Why it's so Hard for White People to Talk about Racism."* Copyrighted by Beacon Press, 2018, in the Foreword Michael E. Dyson classifies *racism as a disease.* Vessel van der Kolk, MD, in his book, *The Body Keeps Score: Brain, Mind and Body In the Healing of Trauma, Penguin Books, 2014; Does not address racism in particular, but* does captivating studies on how the body absorbs trauma from the mind and brain, paralyzing freedom and creativity.*(I mentioned Psoriasis earlier in this book).*

I coined in my thesis "The Mythology of Racism, A TA Perspective," I coined the phrase *"Racosis!"* or pathology. I invite psychiatrists, psychologists or those with degrees, that they already know, to reframe the term *Racism*, which I believe, without proper credentials, to be a *misnomer*. Thanks Ds. Kolk and Diangelo and I'm certain other writers and professors!

An example is appropriate to remember my raising in Winona, MS where it was OK to play children's games between blacks and whites until teenage years. As children (in innocence) we did not notice or forgot skin differences many times until the societal norm (usually 14 years of age) for the separation of human worth on the playground. My sisters played, in exchanged homes, with a white female neighbor throughout childhood and when she reached 14 or 15, in our home, tragedy struck. She said "Suge, I will be fifteen tomorrow, don't you think its time for you and Baby Sister to say "Yes Maam!" to me? Suge

(Rubye) said: "What?" Baby Sister (Geraldine, 2 years younger) said "Ahua!" Tears broke as with redden face she ran down the stairs from our back door and never came to our home again. I remember when seeing her walking toward me on sidewalks, changing sides to not be forced to speak. If she was 14 or 15, Baby Sister was 12 or 13 and I was 11 or 12. Such a painful memory, I soon forgot what she looked like, forever. When I go home, her home and my physical memory of her, my sisters' childhood friend, are gone as though she never lived. Such a human travesty.

REFLECTION, SUMMARY, AND CONCLUSION

Pastors are not totally oblivious to problems that affect their memberships, in their churches and community. And church members are very cognizant of the power their pastors wield over and within their churches and community. Although extremely protective of their pastorate turf and following the dictates of their memberships on church involvement, pastors selectively involve themselves in issues that impact their congregations and community.

An example is when the renaming of public parks in the city of Memphis became a pressing issue for the City Council in July 2005. Because statues of Confederates Jefferson Davis and General Bedford Forrest do not represent the best interest of African Americans, African Americans on the city council pressed for their removal from the public park, paid by public tax dollars. The issue became so inflamed that Reverends Jesse Jackson and Al Sharpton were invited and accepted leading protest marches in Memphis in support of removal of the statues. A local pastor, who also serves as local director of Operation Push, extended the invitation.

In the August 7, 2005 issue of the Commercial Appeal, columnist David Waters wrote an interesting article on pastoral issues in the African American community. Waters acknowledged that we can move churches from one location to the next. Cemeteries are moved to make room for airport runways and shopping malls. "We can move dead babies by the dozens to a potter's in the burps each year." Waters asks, "Why can't we move one graveside?"

He then continues with the fact of Memphis having the highest infant mortality rate among the nation's 60 largest cities or twice the national average. At the time, every 43 hours an infant died in Shelby County. A larger percentage of these babies are African Americans. He asked if anyone called Reverend Al Sharpton about that. He further relates that according to the African American Family Institute, seven of ten births in Shelby County are to unmarried African American women—twice the national average.

In Waters' article, his contention is that half of all African American children in Shelby County live with single parents. He begs the question; did anyone call Reverend Jesse Jackson about that. Tens of thousands of Tennesseans lost their health coverage in July 2005 with the disproportionate number of African American decent. The Southern Christian Leadership Conference held a vigil in Nashville, demonstrating against the decision to eliminate people from the Tenn Care rolls.

The local leader of SCLC, now retired, was also a local pastor, and great by any standard for clergy. However, the demonstrations are reactive rather than proactive, and pastor participation, including myself, especially in Memphis, was non-responsive in confronting serious economic, mismanagement, systemic abuse and political issues which gave opportunity for the Governor's action of cutting the rolls. David Waters only confirms pervasive views of accusations of "too little too late" pastoral involvement. The problems are so enormous that no one discipline can get their arms around it. Regardless of calling.

Though Waters is "sharp shooting" the decision of clergy with national prominence to assist local problems of Memphis, priorities are within questionable limitations. There was not a visible outcry through media from the leadership of the African American community and pastors about the extremely high crime rate, inclusive of murders, robberies, and break-ins which disproportionately plague African American communities. The same has changed today for pastors in African American communities.

The murder rate of Memphis in African American communities set a record during this same period of political fights over removing the statues from the public parks. The solution was postponed when the City Mayor entered the fray and declared his authority as the sole authority for removal of statues. He further reduced such actions as a lesser priority to the acute problems facing citizens of Memphis. Contrastingly, on December 20, 2017 the statues of Nathan Bedford Forrest and Jefferson Davis were removed by the same Mayor, under much criticism. However, the move has been legally validated by courts at the highest State level.

Nevertheless, although pastors are involved through their churches and community schools, from lack of media coverage, the incidents are examples that only when issues become a media event do, they attract strong intervention of many African American pastors and their white counterparts.

On August 12, 2005, it was reported that more than 60 clergy and laity attended a prayer vigil at Christ United Methodist Church. The vigil was also organized by the local pastor and leader of the Southern Christian Leadership Conference. In all instances, the symbolism compares with at least two scriptures: One in (Jonah 1:13, KJV) where a storm was caused by a disobedient prophet who was attempting to hide from God. The other in (Mark 4:38, KJV) where success to combat a storm was realized only when the disciples asked for intervention by Jesus.

Earlier in this book I referenced the insights from Transactional Analysis. Eric Berne describes human behavior in the language of games and scripts. In his book, *Beyond Games and Scripts edited by Graham Barnes,* he defines a game as *"An ongoing series of complementary ulterior transactions progressing toward a well-defined, predictable outcome."* Berne concludes that these repetitions are superficially plausible, with a concealed motivation or a series of moves with a snare or gimmick.[1] In this same book, a script, as defined by Berne, is *"An ongoing life plan formed in early childhood under parental pressure. It is the psychological force which propels the person toward his destiny, regardless of whether he fights it or says it is his own free will."*[2] He further describes games to be segments of scripts. Scripts belong in the realm of transference phenomena or adaptations of infantile reactions and experiences. But he says, *"a script is not a mere transference reaction for it is an attempt to repeat in derivative form a whole transference drama,* often split up into acts, exactly like theatrical scripts which are intuitive artistic derivatives of those primal dramas of childhood."*[3]

In *Structure and Dynamic of Organizations and Groups by Berne,* chapter six is entitled, "The Birth of a Nation."[4] Berne describes the process for individuals to become a group rather than a party. When America was founded, with the embodiment of the Articles

---

[1] Berne, *Beyond Games and Scripts,* 69.

[2] Ibid., 350.

[3] Ibid., 126.

[4] Berne, *Structure and Dynamic of Organizations and Groups,* 92.

of Confederation, America had the structure of a party rather than a group. There was no internal apparatus for collecting taxes or regulating interstate relations. There was no external apparatus for to protect the country from invasion, from internal aggressions by Native Americans whose country had been taken, or from interference on the high seas. Internal disturbances from individual rivalry and external threats prevented peace from being a reality. The Constitution was drawn up as a remedy. In the process, each member state had to resign some of its individual proclivities in favor of group cohesion.[5]

My rationale for using the language of games and scripts is, first, to emphasize that resolution for resolving problems plaguing African Americans are repetitive. The white child is born with environmental support of world superiority and domination just because of his race. The African American experience is a continued "Reconstruction" era. The black child is born and enveloped in an environment where he is forced to compete for the recognition just for being. Concessions are made by the Congress at the height of demonstrations and national and international media attention to alleviate pain due to racial discrimination. But from greed, mismanagement of resources, or politically negotiated power plays, the effects are minimized.

After winning the fight for affirmative action, percentages on employment and loans, it's interesting how even white women, who are not a minority population, could be used for jobs/loans and student population credit in affirmative action cases. This is not an attack on white women. They too, like black and other women, have been "abused and scorned" in a white male dominated society. Some white males will disagree with such domination. Yet it is not the women who did the lynching. It was not the women who forced racial segregation. It was not the women who destroyed each reconstruction era attempt

---

[5] Ibid., 92-93.

nonwhites made to establish their own upscale businesses with comparative family homes. Such instances were employed to water down the impact of Civil Rights gains for non-whites while enlarging the economic pie of the already advantageous white family. Energies were used only to protect the erosion of white favor until another social eruption reaches crisis proportions again to force another concession.

The process adjusts to repeat itself as is in Berne's description of games and scripts. The formula is as follows: Con + Gimmick Leads to a Response (R) that Leads to a Cross-up (X) that Leads to a Bad Feeling Payoff (BFP). *A game is defined as:" An ongoing series of complimentary social transactions, ulterior in nature, and progressing toward a bad feeling payoff or depression".* Berne describes it best in his "Hello" book where he defines "Over and Over" scripts. He uses Sisyphus of Greek Mythology who was condemned to roll a heavy stone up a hill, and just as he was about to reach the top, the stone rolled back, and he had to start over again.[6] In terms of ultimate failure in the alleviation of social problems, such strategies blend into Shakespearian reproductions of "Much to do About Nothing."

A classical book written by fellow Mississippian Richard Wright entitled *The Outsider still* raises the question about whether America is too invested in being a party rather than a group or nation. This is a party where every individual grouping other than of African ancestry is invited to openly share the benefits. The 20th century examples where Cubans with European traits are accepted at our ports in the state of Florida but those with African traits were returned to Havana. This is a party where boat people from Haiti are returned in masse while Mexicans have become "the largest minority group" in America, which to one group is a problem because they did not follow their party lines in terms of voting at the poles. This a party where immigrants of color

---

[6] Ibid., 206.

have extreme difficulty while those from European nations are readily welcomed. This is a party where those arrested with crack cocaine pay large fines or serve lengthy prison terms while those with cocaine or heroin or found in possession of methylamine or with methylamine lavatories in their homes or businesses are given lighter sentences.

This is a party where petty thieves have the "books thrown at them" in courts, but those whose embezzlements or inside trading schemes negatively affect a lifetime of retirement investments of thousands of citizens, receive shorter sentences in minimum security prisons or are restricted to their luxury homes. Such scripts could not have been better written for H.S. Chamberlain, Robert Wagner or Arthur Gobineau.

John F. Blumenback, an 18th century German is claimed by Rudolph Winsor in his book, "From Babylon to Timbuktu," to be the first to classify people according to skin color. No citizen was hyphenated. The ancients identified people according to their national or tribal name. Let's accept his classification as purely scholastic without racial intent. However, it provided a base to unite people of different colors with *optional* vicious or purely *scholastic* intent.

To live in and not fight against a myth is to create and prolong the negative results of what otherwise could be another Garden of Eden. Don't say it cannot happen. Jesus said, "Thy kingdom come, thy will be done, *on earth* as it is in heaven." (Matthew 6:10, KJV) In his teachings, we have the formula for this creation. It is not a cyclic pattern where evil repeats itself, but peace instead is placed on a continuum track.

Thomas Gosset writes: "In 1880 when the furor of nationalism was high in Germany, H.S. Chamberlain and German nationalist and composer, Richard Wagner, exalted race to the status of religion.[7]

---

[7] Thomas F. Gossett, *Race: The History of an Idea in America* (New York: Shocken Books, 1973), 347.

Chamberlain, an Englishman, became the first to claim Jesus as a member of the Teutonic race and was the first to ascribe Teutonic blood to all great men of other nations.[8] Gosset writes that by 1910, Chambelain's writings had already gone through eight editions and had sold more than 60,000 copies.

However, similar arguments for white superiority were not distributed in America until the late 19th and early 20th century. Thomas Gossett says Chamberlain's work was not published in America until 1911. He further notes that although J.A. Gobineau's, "Essay on the Inequality of the Races," (1853-1855) had been circulated in abbreviated form by White Southerners to defend slavery in 1865; it was not fully translated and published in America until 1910. In 1916, *The Passing of the Great Race* was published in America by Madison Grant. Gosset further contends that "Grant's book marked the turning point from previous indifference among Americans to the immense importance of racial differences."[9] In his early race theories, Gosset supports the notion of author Rudolph Winsor that race was not a problem for ancient people.

Winsor went further and about ancient civilizations, he makes this statement: "If race ever was the original basis of caste in India, it did not remain so. In Greek civilization, we find that there was apparently no relationship between slavery and race. In neither Greece nor Rome does there appear to be much prejudice against Africans because of their race. . . In the thirteenth century, we find an indication of how far the middle Ages were from the idea of race prejudices. In France, Pierre Dubois proposed that more sensible than the Crusades against the Moslems would be intermarriage.[10]

---

[8] Ibid., 348.

[9] Ibid.

[10] Ibid., 7-9.

Grant's assertion is not proof that color prejudices in America were not already deeply rooted during American slavery. Each agrees in their writings that emphasize that the systematization of so-called white racism is a problem of modern creation. Barry N. Schwartz and Robert Disch, in their book, *White Racism,* state that:

From 1619 to about 1660, a period of primary importance in the history of America, America was not ruled by color. Some, perhaps all, of the first group of African Americans worked out their terms of servitude and were freed. During this era *black citizens* were accumulating property, pounds, and indentured servants. One *black* immigrant imported a white man and held him in servitude. The breaking of the bonds of community between black and white Americans began with a conscious decision by the power structures of colonial America. In the 1660's, men of power in the colonies decided that human slavery, based on skin color, was to be the linchpin of the new society.[11]

It may be that racism today is a script or life plan embedded in decisions made in the infancy of our nation. It may be further described as belonging to an adaptation of infantile reactions and experiences. Since then, according to Berne, games are segments of scripts, or the moves by which scripts are carried out, there is a way out.

A powerful design to demonstrate the movement of games was developed by Transactional Analyst, Steve Karpman. Karpman's concept showed a triangle with arrows showing movement in both directions.[12] The characters on the triangle are Victim, Persecutor and Rescuer. All three are dependent upon each other for resources to play their game of choice. Hence, if there is nobody to rescue, the Rescuer

---

[11] Barry N. Schwartz and Robert Disch, *White Racism* (New York: Dell Publishing Company, Inc., 1970), 257-258.

[12] Barnes, *Transactional Analysis*, 18.

will become either a victim or persecutor so that he can switch roles later to satisfy the needs of being a Rescuer. If the Victim is not being victimized, he will find a persecutor or someone to rescue, who has no need for rescue, to experience the place of victim. However, the Persecutor, if he has no victim, will become either victim or rescuer themselves to, and at the appropriate time, become Persecutor again. Karpman shows this as a vicious triangle and the diagnosis is pathology.

One of the primary reasons people play games, according to Berne, is to structure their time. They know of nothing better to do with their lives. The way out of the game, of course, the cure for this insanity, is to get off the triangle. The cure is to neither play the role of Victim, Rescuer or Persecutor.

In Berne's Little Red Riding Hood scrip, Karpman's triangle may assist in the reduction of rape and many other interpersonal crimes. Berne describes the carelessness of the mother, who sent her child, alone, through wolf penetrated woods; the naive daughter who did not notice the characterization differences of her grandmother and a wolf, even after examination; a grandmother who would get in the bed leaving her home with open doors, knowing wolves were prowling around. He classifies the wolf as perhaps being the only innocent victim for not knowing the danger of associating with naive maidens.

While I was a Senior Vice President at Methodist Healthcare, in Memphis, on November 14, 2003, the Norfleet Executive held a forum at the University of Memphis. In assessing the Memphis and Shelby County area, the forum presented the following statistics:

- Memphis is the unhealthiest city in the nation for women
- Memphis is on the bottom 6% of those who exercise
- Memphis is below the national average for healthy eating
- Memphis is above average for BMI's at 27.3

- There is an epidemic of diabetes in the Memphis and Shelby County area
- The mid-South must be educated about exercise, diet and obesity
- The community must take the lead in educating the public about the relationships between diet, exercise, diabetes and obesity

The University of Tennessee Health Science Center's (UTHSC) in 2003 reported on racial comparisons of health. At the Norfleet Forum, included in the UTHSC report to the forum on "The Diabetes Epidemic In Tennessee," page 15 is the following quotation: "The poor and black populations contract most of the diseases associated with diabetes at earlier ages, suffer from these diseases more frequently and die from them sooner than any other Tennessee residents."

In the Selma to Montgomery Civil Rights March of 1965, when I arrived at Selma with a bus load of my fellow seminarians from The Interdenominational Theological Center in Atlanta, this is what we saw as described by David Abernathy: *He (Martin) and I were on the front row with a Greek Orthodox patriarch between us, decked out in all his ecclesiastical regalia, his beard flowing down to his waist. On my right were a group of nuns in their black and white habits, and immediately behind me were two rabbis. We were as ecumenical a group as ever gathered in this country.* [13]

This sea of well-dressed citizens included clergy dressed in different color clergy shirts with white turned collars and business suits. Assembled inside and outside the Brown Chapel AME Church of Selma, people white and black, young and old, male and female, from

---

[13] Ralph David Abernathy, *And the Walls Came Tumbling Down* (New York: Harper and Row Publishers, 1989), 339-340.

East, West, South and North, were a powerful representation of the Church. It has been evaluated that this group, diversity at its highest form, helped to turn the tide of our country from a disgraceful, racist dominating past into public favor of civil rights for all citizens. This diverse body was led by pastors from all over the United States and Canada.

The black and white churches and communities of America, like in the Civil Rights era, are postured with a reservoir of information on racial abuse or disparities in health, housing, education and economics. The United States Department of Public Health has the systemic resources and legal responsibility to eliminate health disparities and disease.

However, without the interracial coming together of churches and other religious institutions of the same mind and spirit, and, the entire communities of laity, and atheists and agnostics within our nation, joining these resources with total commitment to effectively treat and eliminate these disparities, the problem will persist.

Like Sisyphus, under threat or immediate guilt, the ball of true democracy will be pushed almost to the top until the psychological game of choice is played and the process is repeated. And this time, with the assault weaponry and nuclear weapons displayed by people with intelligence on all sides, the earlier destruction of Civil War in America will be incomparable.

In chapter 3 of my doctoral dissertation, (The Participation of Pastors in the Elimination of Disparities in the African American Communities, May 2005, Dayton Theological Seminary, Dayton Ohio, May 2005) I asked Dr. James Cone for ideas on eliminating racism and health disparities of African Americans in the 21st century. His answer was to *"reframe the dialogue on racism for elimination of the same in the 21st century, and to do that he said that blacks and whites must talk to each other; The same must listen to each other; A third point is we must act."*

The developing insights from faith and health conclusions, with emphasis of body, mind and spirit must prevail with action for the total community, or racism through health disparities and other forms will survive another century as well.

To solve the devastating problem of racism, Dr. Martin Luther King, Jr. remains inspirationally prophetic in the echoes of American preaching. His "I have a Dream" address is respected worldwide for freedom loving people.

I believe it is time to break the cyclic racial movements in the histories of major religious denominations. For example, the devastating split in 1844 of the Methodist Episcopal Church into Northern and Southern bodies was over the issue of slavery. Bishop Andrew, a Georgian, owned slaves through inheritance and his wife was also a slaveholder. Because the laws of Georgia prevented them from freeing their slaves, the bishop refused at his conference to desist in the exercise of his office while he remained a slaveholder. Outraged by the actions of the conference, the southern delegates rebelled and left the General Conference of 1844 to go home and organize their own church.[14]

By 1965, Mead asserts that "About 87 percent of Black Christians in America were either Baptist or Methodist with Baptist comprising 65 percent of that numbers. I ask that the so-called racial issues which forged the racial separations of black and white Christians no longer remain an abomination to the body of Christ. Prior to the arrest of Jesus, his prayer was for the oneness of his disciples. John 17:23a (KJV) records these words of Jesus, "I in them, and thou in me, that they may be made perfect in one." NIV translates the same verse: "May they be brought to complete unity." I ask, which is better? To take a knee or spit on the Call of Jesus for oneness?

---

[14] Frank S. Mead, *Handbook of Denominations in the U.S.* (Nashville, TN: Abingdon Press, 1995), 197.

Though believers were to become divided for other than racial issues as well, the notion of racial supremacy is a tragic thorn in the flesh of the Church, weakens its theology of interpersonal relationships, and needs to be eradicated to assist the racist healing of the American society.

The late Reverend Frank Roughton Harvey is an Elder of the United Methodist Church, renowned biblical actor and friend, since 1973. Frank is another angel God placed in my pathway at a most critical time. Frank was invited to Fort Hood to reenact the Lord's Supper dressed in the European version of Jesus.

Frank perfected in full dress the character as he did 13 other biblical characters. However, still racially sensitive, when it came to the foot washing ceremony for Fort Hood Chaplains sitting in a semicircle, Frank on his knees recited the narrative while washing each of our feet, I decided to decline. I was not going to take off my military boot for this naturally red haired, freckled faced, white Georgia boy, thinking he looked like Jesus, to wash my foot. When he reached my location, he was reciting Peter's response of: "Thou shall never wash my feet!" (John 13:8). Looking into my eyes, Frank repeated: "If I do not wash you…" I pulled off my socked boot, angered by watery eyes.

After the service I confessed my plight to Frank. We became instant friends and as I got promoted in rank, I contracted Frank to perform in all my assignments in Korea, Germany, Memphis and Fort Gordon, GA. As the 3rd Infantry Division Chaplain in Germany, I invited Frank to be our Dr. Martin Luther King resource speaker to discuss Dr. King from the perspective of a "Southern White Georgia Boy." When he confirmed in September of that year for January presentations, he had researched all the works in Morehouse and Atlanta University libraries and the MLK Memorial. Ecstatically he called to thank me for introducing him to "One of the greatest persons of our century!"

Frank was superb throughout our Division. Some members of the planning committee were miffed because I had invited a white man to lead MLK celebrations, agreed in the meeting an additional objective was to illustrate that Dr. King had transcended the myth of racial superiority or inferiority. Frank emphasized that Dr. King spoke with truth to create a higher objective of universal peace.

In his thousands of international presentations as the Centurion, Frank proclaims *"It is not new information to pastors, regardless of race, that Christianity is a racially inclusive religion."* Frank's stated conviction is that anything less is a hybrid robbed of the power of the life changing influence of Jesus Christ. In Franks drama as the Centurion, Frank's quote is as follows:

Y'shua struggled and slithered along until a black African lunged from the crowd with a gesture of compassion on his face. The Centurion of Franks presentation confessed: "I tapped my spear on the shoulder of that black Cyrenian whom we later learned was named Simon. That was the gesture we used in commandeering a civilian to carry our military burden for a mile. Simon untied the beam and carried the Savior's cross to the top of the mountain. It was the only gesture of compassion that really helped him on that day of infamy. Later when Christianity began to spread, that same Cyrenian was amazed that people had seen Y'shua alive after his crucifixion. He said I know that man. I carried his cross! He became a convert. Paul and the Christian brotherhood affectionately called him Simon the Niger. Translated from the Greek it means Simon the Black. His son Rufus was convinced and converted along with two other black Cyrenians, Barnabas and Lucius. They became prophets and teachers in the church at Antioch. God's vision to restore humanity, as an inclusive family got off to a good start in the very foundation of the church. You can't get more foundational than to carry the savior's cross to share his burden on the day he was crucified. The Church had a Jerusalem headquarters for evangelizing the Jews. However, the headquarters for restoring God's inclusive and universal vision was at Antioch. Paul put Simon the black Cyrenian and his son Rufus in charge of the teaching there. It is ironic that a militant religion tries to lure people of color away from Christianity with the argument that Christianity is the white man's religion. What makes it so ironic is that two black Africans were the professors of the first seminary Christianity ever had.[15]

According to (Acts 11:19-26, KJV), the Christian community at Antioch began when Christians, who were scattered from Jerusalem, because of persecution, fled to Antioch. They were joined by Christians from Cyprus and Cyrene who migrated to Antioch. It was in Antioch that the followers of Jesus were first referred to as Christians. (Wikipedia, Free Encyclopedia)

After the devastating impact of Hurricane Katrina on the Gulf Coast in August 2005, on September 3, the Memphis City Mayor called for a meeting of pastors, political and business leaders to Mississippi Boulevard Christian Church. The goal was announced to raise $10m

---

[15] Frank Roughton Harvey, "The Roman Centurion," One Man Biblical Drama. Produced and directed by Frank Harvey, 1973. Videocassette.

"through local congregations and businesses that will be distributed to hurricane victims staying in the Memphis area."[16] Officials urged local clergy to open their doors to those seeking refuge in Memphis and to work with relief efforts.

To me, it is significant that in crisis, the Mayor did not call to African American pastors but through all media available, sent a call to clergy from "all houses of worship" in the Memphis area. More than 500 religious leaders attended the meeting. The racial, ethnic and religious diversity of their representation could parallel the same in Selma during the year 1965 that turned the tide of Civil rights in America. The Mayor singled out a pastor's visit that energized him to action. Pastors by virtue of divine providence and history are extremely influential people. The same could parallel the Pentecostal experience of 1st century A.D.

I remember when black and white United Methodist Conferences of Mississippi were in the thick of plans for merger. The General Conference had voted to racially desegregate the jurisdictions in 1968. Blacks and whites were positive and negative on both sides of voting for it to happen at the Conference levels. In one of our meetings of the North Mississippi Conference, I remember an important statement by Reverend Roy D. McAllily whose son is now a United Methodist Bishop. Roy said, *"Every now and then I say: "If I were not a United Methodist" ... (and then I think of all our many church holdings, resources and ministries) ... and reemphasizing each positive work of our Methodist Church, he concludes: "If I were not a United Methodist, I'd just be shame!!"*

To our Upper Mississippi Annual Conference, before our racial desegregating vote in 1968, Dr. Major Jones, President of Gammon Theological Seminary preached a sermon on "Just Right." *He compared*

---

[16] James Davis, "Memphis Relief Drive Shoots for $10 Million," *The Commercial Appeal*, 3 September 2005, sec. 1A, p.1,8.

the worship patterns of blacks and whites: "Blacks stay too long; whites don't stay long enough but when we get together, we will be just right. In church administration, whites spend too much time; blacks don't spend enough but when we get together, we will be just right. In meditation, blacks don't spend enough time; whites spend too much time but when we get together, it will be just right."

In the 21st century, with the re-segregation of many of our churches along racial lines, it appears that we don't want to be "Just right" or spiritually or biblically "right" Christians. We prefer seemingly to be culturally or politically "right." The creations of cultural and political platforms have material payoff objectives in mind. We might ask the Pharisees and Sadducees where it placed them on the future agenda of Jesus.

Now is the time to reverse a racial stigma created by the evil clutches of racism on health, economic, social, educational and political disparities. The Church Hospital Network (now Congregational Health Network) inspired by CEO Gary Shorb, developed at Methodist Healthcare South Hospital under Hospital Administrator Joe Webb is a model for "eating the elephant of racism," one bite at a time through increasing participation of pastors, across racial, denominational and religious barriers, to address health disparities in the economically deprived communities (neighborhoods). As the "bell tolls" for the African American community (neighborhoods), in terms of healthcare and other opportunities to the American dream, it also tolls for the entire American community.

Healthcare is just one critical area of exercising one's right in a wealthy democratic republic. I thank God that the Affordable Healthcare plan, praised for years by Americans for Europe and Canada, is now available but also under vigorous political attack for all Americans amid constant political protest for suspicious reasons.

If the poor are expected to fight our wars; work the under wage value jobs; invest in the most unappreciated values in properties; forced into the less prestigious schools and colleges and thereby forced into the lesser quality of healthcare providers, and then for the needed recruits in our armed forces, hi-tech industries and better prepared families and communities, other than racial, under our American flag, what's the problem? Communism, we fought to destroy, was destroyed as a conquering ideology. Affordable Healthcare should reduce the measurement of distinction and pride in being in only an "upper class" citizenry of our nation. A nation of the people, by the people and for the people must be priority in our 21st century. Anything less in goals and ambition will increase the pathological tragedy of one group perpetuating wars and disaster by preaching one group should rule the world.

In 2001, the CEO of Methodist Healthcare asked me to visit supported hospitals in Moscow and Saint Petersburg, Russia. Maurice, in responding to the National call for Détente between America and Russia, offered Methodist Healthcare to assist Russia with curing cancer in children. In partnership with St. Jude Children's Hospital, the cancer rate after 10 years was reduced to the level of cure at St. Jude in America.

In my week there, our driver was a retired Russian Army Sergeant. When saying our goodbyes, with teary eyes he said: *"Davis, you and me, as soldiers, for years, without knowing each other, trained to fight to kill each other. Now you and me, black and white, are now friends. You must come back and we can go into the woods and talk and eat rabbits together."* Then with a Sergeant and Chaplain hug, we departed. Thanks Maurice Elliott and the United Methodist Church for what must be and can be done in America between a contrived connotation: *races and nations.*

In 2001, my CEO, Maurice Elliott invited me to take a Pediatrician,

Health Nurse and a Community Specialist and visit Africa University in Zimbabwe, Africa for a feasibility study on setting up a clinic to deal with the AIDs crisis. St. Jude had received approval government approval (FDA) to test an Anti-HIV vaccine. The clinic was successful with added bringing of nurses, science teachers and physicians to the USA for partnership research and cure.

The collaboration between Methodist Healthcare, the St. Jude Children's Research Hospital and Africa University has yielded and continues to yield considerable benefits with regard to public health. Initially articulated around the testing of a potential vaccine for HIV/AIDS, there were a total of 28 African health care professionals—doctors, nurses and public health officials—in infectious diseases management. These professionals received training and exposure in the United States and in Africa and they returned to serve in Zimbabwe and Mozambique. That training/exposure was sponsored by Methodist Healthcare and the St Jude Children's Research Hospital. Under the partnership, St Jude provided funding of approximately $2.5 million towards the development of a clinical research center tied to Africa University's Faculty of Health Sciences (now part of the College of Health, Agriculture and Natural Sciences at Africa University).

This is another example as to how our advancement in medicine can increase solutions to health issues in America and world communities.

There are no minorities in America. There are Americans. Let the 21st century become a time when mental, spiritual, social and physical health become the norm for our American communities.

Many whites have enjoyed world privileges for generations. Less we overlook for political reasons, many whites have lived lower economic privileges than blacks as well. Consequently, overlooking prepared media and studying hard demographic numbers, a very large percentage of whites mirror the percentages of have and have-nots as in every culture. And it is some criminal haves who cultivate and manipulate the anger of those in between to keep those who have become secure, and thereby placed in an admiration society, while the have–nots of all races fight for the crumbs.

For so many years the success of Anglo writers of the late eighteenth century have mythologized the innocence; beauty; military, ownership and personal power; intellectual superiority; wealth; religiosity; "sugar and spice and everything nice," as endowed featured of one people to the subjugation of others. The results are unimaginable horror in the lives of human beings on every continent of our known world. So many whites in any part of the world, whether "Tarzan's" African jungles or "James bond's native or foreign cities, were always sophisticated enough, ideas implanted from birth, to dominate any present foe. And whether in Science fiction movies, beast filled jungles or crisis filled cities, when the scene called for the horrific defeat of a human being, some dark skinned "Black" person with big eyes or scary disposition would most likely be the loser of life and the "White" champ the victor over the evil challenger and one who always walked or rode away with todays' dress size "6 or 7" beautiful female.

Consequently, even as in Vietnam (stated earlier in this book), where Americans were an obvious minority, some of our white and even black soldiers lived and treated South Vietnamese as though they themselves were the majority and superior victors of the earth. And repetitively, it is this supremacy misperception that perpetuates much of our community, our national, and I believe, our world crisis in human relations; and debatably, a *contributing cause for* not clearly winning the war in Vietnam. (In June –August 1967, we were taught in Chaplain Basic Training that "if we don't win the people, we cannot win the war!") America, listen to the classes you have taught in human relations!!!

There are those who will, like the many whites on one side and nonwhites on the other side, who will "burn the hay, although they have no capability of eating it." (Dog in the Manger) Yet there is unwillingness to let others for whom eating hay is a natural food, enjoy the beauty of nature. There are some men (perhaps women) whose imminent domain belief expect submission to themselves of every opposite sex beauty or "handsomeness" they see. Greed beyond sex (Sigmund Freud may say it's the primate drive) does have a comparable operation, which is why marketers use "sex appeal" to sell cars, clothing, medical supplies, movies and, as stated earlier, other goods and racial supremacy.

Before this book ends, another, very intelligent but misguided high school dropout or college educated person has ended their productive life while been used by the NRA and related interests, and other so-called racially sensitive groups who are historically used by politicians and entrepreneurs to control votes and make extravagant money for big business. The creation and sustaining of racial tension sells votes, weaponry, homes, millions of dollars for architects and material makers to build un-needed new schools, churches and other things, while gobbling up necessary farmland; rerouting water ways and redlining older areas while depressing real estate values for the poor until the wealthy and powerful can repurchase low and sell high again.

Will you say this with me? "I know there is no such thing as *racism*!! It is a myth implanted into the heads of anyone needing to justify a reason to exploit or for which to be exploited." Anybody who comes to us talking race or political party, hold on to your pocketbook and your vote. An exploitation is about to take place. The late Governor George

Wallace had a saying that "There's not a dime's worth of difference between a Republican and a Democrat." My position is that there's not a dime's worth of difference between black and white folk, nor human beings all over our world.

Mr. Wallace was developing political capital while running for President of our USA on an Independent ticket. Before his death, I read in media where he apologized to his countrymen and countrywomen for falsifying his racial beliefs. According to one of my seminary classmates, of the Interdenominational Theological Center, Governor Lester Maddox invited, the three of them to the Georgia Governor's mansion to a reconciliation dinner for his "Axe Handle" tactics preventing them from eating in his restaurant.

I may have already mentioned the privilege and difficulty I had in shaking the highly commendatory hand of Senator Strom Thurmond of Georgia when he came as guest speaker for our soldiers at Fort Gordon, GA. We were, since gramma school, taught to respect those appointed to positions of authority. The disappointment is when those selected, abuse their national or community positions, to serve only their neighborhood. Mr. Thurmond very graciously stated how proud he was to have me as Post Chaplain at Fort Gordon. Yet I had difficulty erasing the *racially slurred enunciation imposed on blacks* from vocal memory of his many televised, irresponsible racially slurred speeches prior the Voting Rights Bill enactment. When considering people we have difficulty loving or respect, try this affirmation: "I love him/her as a creature of God and forgive them for the lives they destroyed. They *and* we are in the hands of God, not ours, for eternity. You see I, and you too, have no choice but to one day, (Repeat), to one day meet our Maker.

God made us who we are, and we are neither white nor black. We are the products of the natural environment of our ancestral birth. Out of love God physically protected us from nature. Black folk still do not like freezing cold climates. White folk tolerate heat but must employ chemically products to protect their skin.

Like in the Garden of Eden everything was there for our comfort. But evil has upset the continuity of safety and plenty, and we must ask the original architect and builder for forgiveness and accept the grace offered in Jesus for a King Josiah type of reform of people, lands and care of the environment. Games described by Transactional Analysis have been implemented in our social order. Using the formula of TA, the cure for such game-playing is to neither be a Rescuer, Victim or Persecutor but rather the person of integrity God intended us to be.

"All have sinned and come short of the glory God." (Roman 3:23, KJV) So it's not enough for us to *say that Upper Room quotation with Jesus:* "Lord is it I?" We must go further than "Lord is it I?" with "Brother or Sister is it you?" That's true evangelism. We are in this world together and neither of us cannot stop the show, but as is seen today can "mess up" the pie or dance floor so that it's difficult for others to have pleasurably enjoyment. We can build all the gated and racially segregated communities' developers can design and sell. But there will be no peace until, as stated earlier in this book *by*, Walter Cronkite, "All it takes is a change of heart."

We can segregate the so-called races so that economically and politically contrived schemes have the political power to execute. Tragically, have we forgotten interracial and intra-racial wars and thefts and all types of crimes among all peoples of the world? I remember racial segregation, in the black community, where peacefully, black folk could not walk the streets and senior citizens could not sit on their porches. In yesteryears and today crimes of all sorts ravaged and ravage the white communities but are publicly protected by owning the press. Black folks who worked and work in homes told stories the press was not permitted to print.

We can also attempt to kill or disenfranchise all the identified competitors within our political scopes to protect ascribed manifest destinies. In the end a false notion of safety is again pitifully ignored. The Rapture is not designed to necessarily save us, but to purify the earth. It could be another thousand years or millennials away. Please read the 24 chapter of Matthew. Yet eternal agony or Heaven may be one minute away for us? Three minutes? Ten years? Or a lifetime away? But it is there.

We control nothing!! Those who claim to know the secrets from the book of Daniel or Revelations, or other biblical or religious places, *or as according to Jesus in (Matthew 24, KJV),* have religious freedom to interpret their convictions. American soldiers died and fought to give the right of religious freedom. So, writers write what you will. I did. Readers read what you read. Truth still stands, unassisted and without the need of props or rationalization. I believe, according to Scriptures I read, "Then Peter opened his mouth, and said, of a truth I perceive that God is no respecter of persons:" (Acts 10:34, KJV). I close this book with a Scriptural passage that challenges my remaining faithful to my Call for Christian service. *I also believe this to be a formidable and inclusive pastoral objective for members of their flock. I bring this book to a close with a passage from (Luke 16:20-31, KJV).*

20 And there was a certain beggar named Lazarus, which was laid at his gate, full of sores,

21 And desiring to be fed with the crumbs which fell from the rich man's table: moreover, the dogs came and licked his sores.

22 And it came to pass, that the beggar died, and was carried by the angels into Abraham's bosom: the rich man also died, and was buried;

²³ And …(being in torments in Hades, NKJV) he lifts up his eyes, being in torments, and seeth Abraham afar off, and Lazarus in his bosom.

²⁴ And he cried and said, Father Abraham, have mercy on me, and send Lazarus, that he may dip the tip of his finger in water, and cool my tongue; for I am tormented in this flame.

²⁵ But Abraham said, Son, remember that thou in thy lifetime recievedst (received) thy good things, and likewise Lazarus evil things: but now he is comforted, and thou art tormented.

²⁶ And beside all this, between us and you there is a great gulf fixed: so that they which would pass from hence to you cannot; neither can they pass to us, that would come from thence.

²⁷ Then he said, I pray thee therefore, father, that thou wouldest (would) send him to my father's house:

²⁸ For I have five brethren; that he may testify unto them, lest they also come into this place of torment.

²⁹ Abraham saith unto him, they have Moses and the prophets; let them hear them.

³⁰ And he said, Nay, father Abraham: but if one went unto them from the dead, they will repent.

³¹ And he said unto him, If they hear not Moses and the prophets, neither will they be persuaded, though one rose from the dead.

We cannot place friends, foe, or ourselves in either Heaven or Hades. Eternity is controlled by the way we live out our faith. We must prepare for eternity as we have no control over our doom.

In 1955 our Winona, Mississippi High School choir was invited to sing "Make America Proud of You;" *author of lyrics: Jack Fulton and Lois Steele. Don McNeil's International Breakfast Club of Chicago extended the invitation to us.* The lyrics and music became engraved into my spirit at 15 years of age. The lyrics were so powerful, to me, that subsequently in each Army assignment, I requested of the Commander that the song and music become the unit motto or theme song. Obviously, it never happened because the military has its own historical marching songs.

In retrospect, my neighborhood throughout the years, and the communities where I have professionally lived in and provided services to, have taught me the importance of diversely interacting with all types of people. Churches, schools, adult conversations in cotton fields, barber shops, jobs, all became social rudders guiding me toward maturity. As in this book, I recall ideas surfaced I would have thought to be long forgotten. To God be the glory and may God in His grace inspire grace receiving and grace giving people enough residue to rescue us from our nation and world of moral, religious and economic decline.

BIBLIOGRAPHY

Abernathy, Ralph David. *And the Walls Came Tumbling Down*. New York: Harper and Row, 1989.

Altizer, Thomas J., and William Hamilton. *The Death of God*. Indianapolis, IN: The Bobbs- Merrill Company, Inc., 1966.

American Community Survey Profile. *Population and Housing Profile: Shelby County, TN*. Washington, DC: U.S. Census Bureau, 2003.

Baab, Otto J. *The Theology of the Old Testament: The Faith behind the facts of Hebrew Life and Writings*. Nashville, TN: Abingdon Press, 1959.

Bainton, Roland H. *The Horizon History of Christianity*. New York: American Heritage Publishing, 1964.

Barclay, William. *The Gospel of Mark*. Edinburgh, Scotland: The St. Andrew Press, 1956.

Barnes, Graham, Editor. *Transactional Analysis After Eric Berne*. New York: Harper's College Press. 1977.

Bartlett, David L. *Ministry in the New Testament*. Eugene OR: Wipf and Stock Publishers, 2001.

Bennett, Lerone. *Before the Mayflower, A History of the "African American" in America 1619-1964*. New York: Penguin Books, 1975.

Benor, Daniel J. *Consciousness Bioenergy and Healing.* Medfore, NJ: Wholistic Healing Publications, 2004.

Berk, Stephen E. *A Time to Heal.* Grand Rapids, MI: Baker Books, 1997.

Berne, Eric. *Beyond Games and Scripts.* New York: Grove Press, Inc., 1976.

_____. *Games People Play.* New York: Grove Press Inc., 1964.

_____. *The Structure and Dynamics of Organizations and Groups.* New York: Grove Press, Inc., 1963.

_____. *What do you say after you say hello.* New York: Grove Press, Inc., 1972.

Bevans, Stephen. *Models of Contextual Theology.* New York: Orbis Books, 1985.

Braithwaite, Ronald L. and Sandra Taylor, Editors. *Health Issues in the Community.* San Francisco, CA: Jossey-Bass, 2001.

Branch, Taylor. *Pillar of Fire, America in the King Years 1963-65.* New York: Simon and Schuster, 1998.

Burgess, Diana, Steven Fu, and Michelle van Ryn. "Why do providers contribute to disparities and what can be done about it?" *Journal of General Internal Medicine* 19(11), 2004.

Cashmore, Ellis and James Jennings. *Racism Essential Readings, ed. Ashley Montagu* London: Sage Publications, 2001.

Census 2000 Supplementary Survey Profile. Population and Housing Profile. Available at: http://www.census.gov/acsProducts/Profiles/Single/2000/C2SS/Narrative/ 155/NP1; Internet; Accessed 13 November, 2003.

Centers for Disease Control and Prevention. *Morbidity and Mortality Weekly Report* 50(36), 2001.

Chand, Sarla, Esther Mabry and Dave Hilton. *Abundant Living, Global Health and Christian Response-Ability.* Nashville, TN: General Board of Global Ministries, 2001.

Chu, Susan and Lawrence Baker. "Racial/Ethnic Disparities in Preschool Immunizations: United States, 1996-2001." *American Journal of Public Health* 94(6), 2004.

Cone, James H. *For My People, Black Theology and the Black Church.* Maryknoll, NY: Orbis Books, 1978.

Cone, James H. *God of the Oppressed.* New York: The Seabury Press, 1975.

Cone, James H. *Liberation: A Black Theology of Liberation.* Philadelphia, PA: J. B. Lippincott Company, 1970.

Cone, James H. *Martin & Malcolm & America, A Dream or a Nightmare.* Maryknoll, NY: Orbis Books, 1991.

Cone, James H. *Risks of Faith: The Emergence of Black Theology of Liberation, 1968-1998.* Boston, MA: Beacon Press, 1999.

Cone, James. *Speaking the Truth.* New York: Orbis Books, 1999.

Corey, Gerald. *Theory and Practice of Group Counseling.* Pacific Grove, CA. Brooks: Cole Publishing Company, 1990

Cornell, Bill. "Reflections on the Edinburgh Conference." *The Script ITAA* 35(6), 2005.

Cranton, Patricia. *Professional Development as Transformative Learning.* San Francisco, CA: Jossey-Bass, 1996.

Cummings, Elijah. *Congressional Black Caucus.* Available from http://www.ampute.org /multicultural/connections/section 1-02.html; Internet; Accessed June 2005.

Creswell, John W. *Research Design: Qualitative, Quantitative, and Mixed Methods Approaches,* Second Edition. Thousand Oaks, CA: Sage Publications, 2003.

Dalton, Harlon L. *Racial Healing, Confronting the Fear Between Blacks and Whites.* New York: Anchor Books Doubleday, 1995.

Davies, Richard E. *Handbook for the Doctor of Ministry Project: An Approach to Structured Observation of Ministry.* New York: University Press of America, 1984.

Davis, Elvernice. *Paper for Master s of Divinity Project: The Mythology of Racism: A TA Perspective, ITC, Atlanta, GA 1977*

Davis, Elvernice.Doctoral Dissertation: Elimination of Health Disparities Among African Americans, Dayton Theological seminary, Dayton,OH, 2005

Davis, James. "Memphis Relief Drive Shoots for $10 Million." *The Commercial Appeal,* 3 September 2005.

Dedman, Bill and Stephen Doig. *Newsroom Diversity Report for the Commercial Appeal, Memphis.* Available at: http://powerreporting. com//knight/tn_the_commercial   _appeal_memphis.html; Internet; Accessed June 2005.

Dehaven, Mark J., Irby B. Hunter, Laura Wilder, and James W. Walton. "Health Programs in Faith-Based Organizations: Are they Effective?" *American Journal of Public Health,* 94 (6), 2004.

Department of Health, State of Tennessee. *Fact Sheet: History and Facts about Memphis and Shelby County.* Memphis Shelby County Public Library and Information Center. Available at: http://www.memphislibrary.lib.tn.us/history/ memphis2.htm; Internet; Accessed 10 November 200ibrary

Dupes, Bill. "Reach One, Teach One" in *Connections: The Amputee Coalition of America's Multicultural Publication.* Available from http://www.amputee-coalition.org/multticultural/connections/section1-03.html; Internet; Accessed June 2005

Diangelo, Robin, *White Fragility.* Beacon Press, Boston, 2018.

Edleman, Marian Wright. *Lanterns, A Memoir of Mentors.* Boston, MA: Beacon Press, 1999.

Edmundson, Aimee. "38108 The Infant Death Capital." *The Commercial Appeal,* 13 March 2005.

Essig, Montgomery F. *The Comprehensive Analysis of the Bible.* Nashville, TN: The Southwestern Company, 1951.

Fanon, Frantz. "The Wretched of the Earth." New York: Grove Press, 1961.

Feagan, Joe R. and Melvin P. Sikes. *Living with Racism, The Black Middle Class Experience.* Boston, MA: Beacon Press, 1994.

Fee, Elizabeth. *History and Development of Public Health* in F. Douglas Scutchfield and C. William Keck, Principles of Public Health Practice. Clifton Park, NY: Thompson, Delmar Learning, 2003.

Ferm, Deane William. *Contemporary American Theologies, A Critical Survey.* New York HarperCollins, 1990.

Fischer, David Hackett. *Historians' Fallacies, Toward a Logic of Historical Thought*. New York: Harper & Row, 1970.

Fogel, Joshua. Highlights of the 95th annual meeting of the American Psychopathological Association: Prevention of mental illness. *Medscape Psychiatry and Mental Health,* 10 (1), 2005.

Frank, Jerome D. *Persuasion and Healing*. New York: Schocken Books, 1965.

Franklin, John Hope. *From Slavery to Freedom*. New York: Alfred A. Knopf, Inc., 1988.

Frazier, E. Franklin. *The "African American" Church in America*. New York: Schoken Books, 1974.

Fanon, Frantz. "The Wretched of the Earth." New York: Grove Press, 1963.

Gee, Gilbert and Devon Payne-Sturges. "Environmental Health Disparities: A Framework Integrating Psychosocial and Environmental Concepts." *Environmental Health Perspective 112(17), 2004.*

Gilliland, B., R. James and J.T. Bowman. *Theories and Strategies in Counseling and Psychotherapy*. Boston, MA: Allyn and Bacon Publishers, 1994.

Ginzberg, Eli and Alfred S. Eichner. *Troublesome Presence*. New Brunswick, NJ: Transaction Publishers, 1993.

Gossett, Thomas F. *Race: The History of an Idea in America*. New York: Schocken Books, 1963.

Greenwood, Davydd J. and Morten Levin. *Introduction to Action Research: Social Research for Social Change*. Thousand Oaks, CA: Sage Publication, 1998.

Grembrowski, David. *The Practice of Health Program Evaluation.* Thousand Oaks, CA: Sage Publications, 2001.

Grier, William, and Price Cobbs. *Black Rage.* New York: Bantam Books, 1969.

Harrell, Camara Jules P. *Manichean Psychology.* Washington, DC: Howard University Press, 1999.

Harris, James H. *Pastoral Theology: A Black Church Perspective.* Minneapolis, MN: Fortress Press, 1991.

Harris, Marvin. *Culture, Man, and Nature.* New York: Thomas Y. Cromwell, Inc., 1971.

Harris, Thomas. *I'm OK—You're OK, A Practical Guide to Transactional Analysis.* New York: Harper and Row, Publishers, 1969.

Harvey, Frank Roughton. *The Roman Centurion,* One Man Biblical Drama. Produced and directed by Frank Harvey. 1973. Videocassette.

Herberg, Will. *Four Existentialist Theologians.* Garden City, NJ: Doubleday and Company, 1958.

Hopkins, Dwight, ed. *Black Faith and Public Talk.* New York: Orbis Books, 1999.

Hyatt, James Philip. *The Interpreter's Bible,* vol. 5. Nashville, TN: Abingdon Press, 1956.

Johnson, Kathy Latch. *The Community News Flash.* Available at: http://www.communitynewsflash.com; Internet; Accessed March 2004.

Johnson, Sherman E. *The Interpreters Bible*, vol. 7. Nashville, TN: Abingdon Press, 1951.

Johnson, Walter. *Soul By Soul: Life Inside the Antebellum Slave Market.* Cambridge, MA: Harvard University Press, 2003.

Kegley, Charles W. and Robert W. Bretall, Editors. *Reinhold Niebuhr, His Religious, Social and Political Thought.* New York: The Macmillan Company, 1956.

Knitter, Paul F. *Theologies of Religions.* New York: Orbis Books, 2003.

Kolk,Vessel van der, MD, *The Body Keeps Score: Brain, Mind and Body in the Healing of Trauma, 1ˢᵗ Edition.* Penguin Books, 2014.

Kong, Stephanie H. *A Minute for Your Health.* Roscoe, IL: Hilton Publishing Co., 2003.

Lewis, David. *King: A Critical Biography.* New York: Praeger Publishers, 1970.

Lincoln, C. Eric. *The Black Church Since Frazier.* New York: Schocken Books, 1974.

Lincoln, C. Eric and Lawrence H. Mamiya. *The Black Church in the African American Experience.* Durham, NC: Duke University Press, 1990.

Loury, Glenn C. *The Anatomy of Racial Inequaltiy.* Cambridge, MA: Harvard University Press, 2002.

Mahlangu-Ngcobo, Mankekolo. *100 Ways of Empowering Women.* Baltimore, MD: Gateway Press, 1999.

_____. *Arise, Women in the Ministry.* Baltimore, MD: Gateway Press, 2004.

_____. *To God Be The Glory.* Baltimore, MD: Gateway Press, 1996.

_____. *Wise Words, Men Empowering Men*. Baltimore, MD: Gateway Press, 1998.

Mail, Patricia, Sue Lachenmyr, Elaine Auld, and Kathleen Roe. Eliminating Health Disparities: Focal Points for Advocacy and Intervention. *American Journal of Public Health* 94(4), 2004.

Markham, Roberta H. and Marie L. Waddell. *10 Steps in Writing the Research Paper*. Woodbury, New York: Barron's Educational Series, Inc., 1971.

Mason, T.B. *The Bible and Race*. Nashville, TN: Broadman Press, 1959.

McMillen, S. I. *None of these Diseases*. Old Tappan, NJ: Fleming H. Revell Company, 1968.

Mead, Frank S. *Handbook of Denominations in the U.S.* Nashville, TN: Abingdon Press, 1995.

Mellor, Jennifer and Jeffrey Milyo, "Individual Health Status and Racial Minority Concentration in US and Counties." *American Journal of Public Health* 94(6) .2004.

Miles, Matthew B. and A. Michael Huberman. *Qualitative Data Analysis*. Thousand Oaks, CA: SAGE Publications, 1994.

Miller-Keane. *Encyclopedia and Dictionary*. Philadelphia, PA: W.B. Saunders Company. Sixth Edition.

Mitchell, Henry. *Black Church Beginnings*. Grand Rapids, MI: William B. Eerdmans Publishing Company, 2004.

Morris, G. Scott. *I Am the Lord Who Heals You*. Nashville, TN: Abington Press, 2004.

Myers, William R. *Research in Ministry: A Primer for the Doctor of Ministry Program*. Chicago, IL: Exploration Press, 2000.

North, James. *Freedom Rising*. New York: Macmillan Publishing Company, 1985.

Park, Andrew Sung. *Racial Conflict and Healing*. Maryknoll, NY: Orbis Books, 1996.

_____. *The Wounded Heart of God: The Asian Concept of Han and the Christian Doctrine of Sin*. Nashville, TN: Abingdon Press, 1993.

Park, Eun Chung. *Either Jew or Gentile*. Louisville, KY: Westminster John Knox Press, 2003.

Pender, Nola, Carolyn Murdaugh, and Mary Ann Parsons. *Health Promotion in Nursing Practice*. Upper Saddle River, NJ: Prentice Hall, 2002.

Pinn, Anne H. and Anthony B. Pinn. *Black Church History*. Minneapolis, MN: Fortress Press, 2002.

Plante, Thomas G. and Allen C. Sherman, ed.. *Faith and Health*. New York: The Guilford Press, 2001.

Pohly, Kenneth. *Transforming the Rough Places, The Ministry of Supervision*. Franklin, TN: Providence House Publishers, 2001.

Pope, Donna. *Diversity Committee Workforce Composition Report*. Memphis, TN: Methodist Healthcare, 2004.

Prentiss, Craig R. *Religion and the Creation of Race and Ethnicity*. New York: New York University Press, 2003.

Preston, Libby. *Epidemics*. Available at: http://www.libby-genealogy.com; Internet; Accessed September 6, 2005.

Proctor, Samuel DeWitt. *The Substance of Things Hoped For.* Valley Forge, PA: Judson Press, 1995.

Proctor, Samuel D. and Gardner C. Taylor. *We Have This Ministry, The Heart of the Pastor's Vocation.* Valley Forge, PA: Judson Press, 1996.

Poussaint, Alvin and Amy Alexander. *Lay My Burden Down.* Boston, MA: Beacon Press, 2000.

Raboteau, Albert, J. *Slave Religion, The Invisible Institution in the Antebellum South.* New York: Oxford University Press, 1978.

Roberts, Deotis J. *Black Theology in Dialogue.* Philadelphia, PA: The Westminster Press, 1987.

_____. *Bonhoeffer & King: Speaking Truth to Power.* Louisville: Westminster John Knox Press, 2005.

_____. *Liberation and Reconciliation.* Philadelphia, PA: The Westminster Press, 1971.

Satcher, David. Address at National Baptist Convention, 5 September 2001. Available at: http://www.thebody.com/cdc/news_updates_archive/sep5_01/convention.html; Internet; Accessed May 2005.

Schanzer, Bella M. and Jeffrey A. Morgan. Indigent Men's Use of Emergency Departments over Primary Care Settings. *American Journal of Public Health* (94)6, 2004.

Scutchfield, F. Douglas and C. William Keck. *Principles of Public Health Practice.* Clifton Park, NY: Thomson Delmar Learning, 2003.

Sernett, Milton C. *Afro-American Religious History: A Documentary Witness.* Durham, NC: Duke University Press, 1985.

Schwartz, Barry and Robert Disch. *White Racism*. New York: Dell Publishing, 1970.

Shi, Leiyu, Lisa Green, and Sophia Kazakova. "Primary Care Experience and Racial Disparities in Self-Reported Health Status." *Journal of the American Board of Family Practice* 17(6), 2004.

Simpson, Cuthbert A. *Interpreters Bible, vol.1*, Nashville, TN: Abingdon Press, 1951.

Spencer, Jon Michael. *Sing a New Song*. Minneapolis, MN: Augsburg Fortress, 1995.

Sweet, Leonard I. *Health and Medicine in the Evangelical Tradition*. Valley Forge, PA: Trinity Press International, 1994.

The Center for Health in Tennessee. Workforce Development Fact Sheet February 2003.

Thomas, Owen C. and Ellen K. Wondra. *Introduction to Theology*. Harrisburg, PA: Morehouse Publishing, 2002

ABOUT THE AUTHOR

Biography of Dr. Elvernice "Sonny" Davis, Chaplain (COL), USA Retired. Elvernice "Sonny" Davis, served 3 years as Executive Director for the United Methodist Neighborhood Centers of Memphis, Inc. He joined Methodist Healthcare in 1998 where he served as Senior Vice-President of Health and Welfare Ministries, retiring fully vested after serving seven and one-half years. He has served eight years as a United Methodist Pastor, 30 years as an Active Duty Chaplain in the United States Army, retiring with the rank of Colonel. "Sonny's" military decorations include two Legions of Merits, The Bronze Star and The Air Medal. In Vietnam, he served as Staff and 2/1 Squadron Chaplain of the 4th Infantry Division. In Wurzburg, Germany, he was excited to serve as Division Chaplain of the 3rd Infantry Division, the division of his western movie hero, Audie Murphy. Chaplain Davis was assigned to the Staff and Faculty of the United States Army Chaplain Center and

School where he taught both Chaplain Officer Basic and Advanced Courses. In his second tour of South Korea, he was Command Chaplain of the Army's only Combined Field Army, headquartered in Uijongbu. He served as Command and Post Chaplain at Fort Monmouth, NJ and Fort Gordon, GA. He retired as Command Chaplain for the United States Army Southeast Regional Medical Command and Eisenhower Regional Medical Center with Headquarters at Fort Gordon, GA, where he established a CPE training Center. He received a Bachelor of Arts Degree in Social Science from Rust College, Holly Springs, MS and a Master of Divinity Degree from Gammon Theological Seminary of the Interdenominational Theological Center in Atlanta, GA. Additionally, he received a Master of Arts Degree in Sociology from Long Island University, Brooklyn, NY and is a Postgraduate Fellow of Psychotherapy from Southeast Institute, Chapel Hill, North Carolina. Chaplain Davis and his wife Cynthia received their Doctor of Ministry Degrees from United Theological Seminary, Dayton, OH in 2005 with a special focus in the Black Church and Public Health. His dissertation is entitled, "Participation of Pastors in Addressing Health Disparities of African Americans." Chaplain Davis holds Clinical Certification in the National Association of Forensic Counselors. He is a member of the Military Chaplains Association of the USA. Chaplain Davis is a 2001 graduate of Leadership Memphis. In 2003, he was certified as a Clinical Member of the National Institute of Business and Industrial Chaplains, Inc. In 2004, Chaplain Davis was appointed to the Board of Health Benefits for the Mississippi Conference of the United Methodist Church. He has served as a member of the St. Jude Sickle Cell Advisory Committee and the Life-Blood Board of Directors. April 2004, he was appointed as a member of the Advisory Board for Sustaining Pastoral Excellence, Memphis Theological Seminary. In 2004, he was appointed to the Spiritual and Emotional Care Task Force for the Mississippi Conference to assist victims of Hurricane Katrina and Rita. In January 2008, he and his wife were selected to join forty clergy participants for the three year Sustaining Pastoral Excellence study group. Chaplain Davis is most pleased that while at Methodist Healthcare he was able to coordinate between Methodist Healthcare, St. Jude Research Hospital and Africa University, located in Zimbabwe, the establishment of clinical trials for an FDA approved anti-AIDS vaccine project. While an Army Chaplain, he conducted numerous workshops on "An Understanding of Racism," and as a trainer for "Faith at Work, Inc." which combined the insights of psychotherapy with biblical applications in small group settings. He believes his academic, pastoral and military experiences, during the heat of the Civil Rights Movement and beyond, provide powerful reflections as an overlay with recommended resolutions for contemporary social issues. His conviction about race is that beliefs in racial inferiority or superiority are deeply embedded pathological issues perpetuating social, political and spiritual instability and the predominance of economic chaos, preventing the realization of the kingdom of God. Born in Vaiden and raised in Winona, Mississippi, "Sonny" and Cynthia are proud parents of four adult children and two grandsons, Jalen and Christian Blake. He loves the pastoral ministry, gardening, traveling and golf. He is most pleased and thankful to God for the opportunity in retirement to support Cynthia as a twice appointed District Superintendent in the Memphis Conference of our United Methodist Church.

Just thankful